BREAKFAST WITH JONNY WILKINSON

BREAKFAST WITH JONNY WILKINSON

by Chris England

JOSEF WEINBERGER PLAYS

LONDON

BREAKFAST WITH JONNY WILKINSON
First published in 2006
by Josef Weinberger Ltd
12-14 Mortimer Street, London, W1T 3JJ
www.josef-weinberger.com
general.info@jwmail.co.uk

ISBN 0 85676 296 2

For my father

BREAKFAST WITH JONNY WILKINSON was first presented at the Menier Chocolate Factory, London on 27th April 2006. It was produced by David Babani and Danielle Tarento, and the cast was as follows:

JAKE	Kevin Wathen
DAVE	Norman Pace
EXLEY	Chris England
NINA	Beth Cordingly
MATT	Michael Beckley
NIGEL	Tony Bell
LENA	Abi Tucker

Directed by Jonathan Lewis
Designed by Anthony Lamble
Lighting design by Tim Mascall
Sound design by Gareth Owen for Orbital

Author's note

The brief snatches of commentary referred to in the script are based on a mixture of the original live commentaries on the match by John Taylor (television coverage) and Ian Robertson (on the radio).

As well as the original cast and crew, I would also like to thank Arthur Smith, Michael Garner, Suranne Jones, Dan Fredenburgh, Nick Court, Cate Debenham-Taylor, Stephanie Langton, David Solomon, Adam Speers, Rebecca Nelson and Lucy McNally for their help in getting the show off the ground.

The Menier Chocolate Factory is a full time producing house and was taken over in February 2004 by Danielle Tarento and David Babani and comprises a theatre, restaurant, bar and rehearsal rooms.

Chocolate Factory awards to date include Theatregoer's Choice Awards 2005 and 2006 for Best Off West End Production (*Fully Committed* and *Sunday In The Park With George*), Peter Brook Empty Space Award 2005 for Upcoming Venue, Critics' Circle Award 2006 for Best Design (*Sunday In the Park With George*) and the Evening Standard Theatre Awards 2005 – Milton Schuman Award for Outstanding Newcomer.

"There's nowhere quite like the Chocolate Factory anywhere . . . the bubbliest kid on the block and one of London's greatest theatre hopes." – The Daily Telegraph

For any further information please contact:

office@menierchocolatefactory.com

or visit www.menierchocolatefactory.com

Tel: 020 7378 1712

Directors:	**David Babani & Danielle Tarento**
Marketing & Box Office:	**Lucy McNally**

ACT ONE

Scene One

JAKE WHITTAM, *a young lad in rugby kit, is in the middle of the rugby field – represented by a spotlit section right at the front of the stage. He crouches to place an imaginary ball carefully on a little ring support. He is focusing, concentrating on the kick.*

JAKE   What would Jonny do . . . ?

              (*Stands now behind the ball and looks up. He bends to pick up some grass and throws it up in the air to check wind. Grass falls straight to floor. He rolls his head round on his neck.*)

              Visualise. Left boot connecting perfectly, the ball spinning end over end, bisecting the sticks perfectly, heading straight for . . . that girl in the crowd, blonde hair, red jumper, it's the girl from the fitness centre in town. She catches it, she smiles, she waves . . .

              (*He enjoys the imaginary success, then snaps himself out of it.*)

              All right, let's do it. Crowd cheering – shut them out.

              (*Does Wilkinson's trademark retreat to his starting position. Step, step, step. Side step, side step. Clasps his hands in front of him, as Jonny does.*)

              Concentrate now, in the groove, into the zone. Focus every nerve, every muscle, every single cell of your body on getting this ball over the bar and between the posts. Nothing left to chance, every factor taken into consideration, just like Jonny Wilkinson . . .

              (*Exhales slowly, then runs up and makes the kick. He holds his finishing position with*

*supreme confidence for a moment. His face
slowly falls as he watches the ball skew off to
the side.*)

Except . . . that I'm not Jonny Wilkinson,
obviously . . .

(*Quick blackout.*)

Scene Two

*Lights up on Greyhawks Rugby Club bar. It is an old-fashioned
wood-panelled affair, bar itself with optics and a couple of stools in
the back corner. Windows along some of the back wall, and a door
leading to the pitches outside and to the car park. A door behind the
bar, stage right, leads to an office, while to stage left there is another
leading to the changing rooms and toilets.*

DAVE DOWSON *is busying himself opening the bar. He is the club
chairman, proud of the position and of the club, which is his little
empire, and he wears a club blazer and tie (and other clothes). He
belongs in the vast grey area that is middle age.*

*Suddenly a rugby ball crashes in through a skylight and bounces
around on the floor.*

DAVE	Christ all-fuck-buggering-mighty!
	(DAVE *clutches his heart, staggers to a seat. He's had quite a shock, and sits down heavily, breathing hard. After a beat he gets to his feet and comes into the middle of the room to look up at the damage.* JAKE *comes in at a trot through the door at the back of the room from the direction of the pitches. He guiltily checks out the broken glass on the floor.*)
JAKE	Sheesh! (*He pulls a face, sheepish.*) Sorry, sorry, Mr Dowson.
DAVE	Phew, Jake, it's you.

JAKE	I've been here since six, Mr Dowson. Couldn't sleep, so I thought I'd come down and kick for a couple of hours. I'm really sorry.
DAVE	All right, all right . . . I dare say Jonny Wilkinson's hit a skylight or two in his time.
JAKE	(*peers up at the ceiling*) I'll get a bit of hardboard on it, or something.
	(DAVE *fiddles with some heaters, spread around the room. Switches them off, then crouches down to feel the carpet.*)
DAVE	OK, good lad, good lad. Actually, you can give me a hand with these first. Over there, look. Still a bit moist, but I shouldn't think anybody will really notice.
JAKE	You opening up, Mr Dowson?
DAVE	Certainly am. What'll you have?
JAKE	(*frowns, puzzled*) No, nothing, it's just that I thought . . .
DAVE	What? That the club wouldn't be open on the biggest day for English rugby in twelve years? Possibly the biggest ever, touch wood? The biggest day for English sport since Ben Cohen's uncle was England's right back in '66. Touch wood.
JAKE	I don't know why . . . I must have just made a mistake.
DAVE	This place will be packed out, even more than last Sunday. It'll start filling up any minute. (*Checks watch, nervous.*) Can you give me a hand with the big screen? Just make sure it doesn't snag on the photos on the way down.
	(JAKE *stands front of stage and mimes guiding the screen into position on the fourth wall, as* DAVE

presses a button behind the bar. There is an electrical whine accompanying this.)

JAKE   Righto, Mr D. (*Looks at screen curiously.*) Is this new?

DAVE   Oh yeah. Bit of a mishap with the old one last week. Bit of spillage. And then it got torn up. And burnt . . . Hey, I might set a new bar record today, you know, especially if England win. That'll give the committee something to think about tomorrow. Eh?

JAKE   It's tomorrow, is it?

DAVE   Yeah, D-Day. Should be quite a weekend, one way or the other.

JAKE   Who's gonna win, do you think?

DAVE   Ah, well, it'll be close. Bob's with me, and Waldron, and Brian, and The Wanker. Toad's with Matt, obviously, and so's Colin and Alan. Nigel's absent, of course, down under. There's a couple of undecideds. Nina for one . . .

JAKE   The rugby, I meant.

DAVE   Oh well, Martin Johnson, he's forgotten how to lose, hasn't he?

JAKE   I wish I had a vote, I wouldn't vote for Matt. He's got the whole team to call me Wilko, now, after last week.

DAVE   Eight out of eight, lad, can't do better than that. Oh, now that reminds me, I've got something to show you. I was going through some of my dad's stuff and I found this. Here . . .

(*From a bag* DAVE *rather reverently and gently takes an old-style rugby shirt.*)

JAKE   This is your dad's?

DAVE	No, no, it was mine, actually. I was an international squad trialist, scrum half. England Probables versus England Possibles.
JAKE	(*impressed*) Really?
DAVE	At Twickenham, it was, on a Tuesday afternoon. I was supposed to get the day off, but Jackson, my headmaster back then, would only give me a half day, so I got there a bit hot and bothered and I didn't really do myself justice, but still. Good day. This is my shirt from that day. A Possible, I was. Never became a Probable.
	(JAKE *fingers the material curiously.*)
JAKE	Wow. They really used to make them in those days, didn't they?
DAVE	Oh yeah, you could make a hammock out of that. (JAKE *hands the shirt back, but* DAVE *holds up his hands.*) I want you to have it.
JAKE	What?
DAVE	Have it. Keep it. It would mean a lot to me.
JAKE	No, Mr Dowson, I couldn't. It's . . .
DAVE	Go on. I'll tell you. You're going to have quite a collection one day, son, international shirts, too, not just "possibles".
JAKE	(*embarrassed*) No, go on, what are you talking about . . . ?
DAVE	Hey, put it on.
JAKE	Eh? No. Maybe later . . .
DAVE	No, go on. It's all right, I washed it.
JAKE	OK. OK . . .

(JAKE *puts the shirt on, a little warily, but once it is on he is pleased with it.*)

DAVE   Yeah, 1981 it was, I remember it well. If only there'd been an England Really Bloody Unlikelies team, I'd have got loads of shirts . . . There, hey, marvellous, it fits you quite well, doesn't it? Mind you, I was a scrawny little streak of piss myself in those days. Maybe it'll bring us luck today, eh?

JAKE   Yeah. Thanks, thanks Mr Dowson.

DAVE   Dave. We're not at school now.

JAKE   Dave. OK, Mr Dowson. Dave. Anyway, anyway, look, I'll just nip up and have a look at the skylight, shall I? (*He goes.*)

DAVE   Right you are.

(*Something needs* DAVE'S *attention at floor level, and he ducks out of sight.* BILL EXLEY, *journalist, somewhere in the 35-45 range, not especially kempt, wanders into the deserted clubhouse. He looks around somewhat disdainfully, undoes his coat, and, after a moment's thought to compose himself he talks into a little tape recorder.*)

EXLEY   At the ungodly hour of eight-fifteen in the morning I found myself in a . . . dilapidated shithole. No, no . . . the retro-chic clubhouse of the Greyhawks rugby union football club.

(*DAVE pops his head up from behind the bar to see who is talking. He and* EXLEY *look at each other for a beat.*)

EXLEY   (*continues talking into tape recorder*) The place seemed deserted, at first, but then a muscular, middle-aged hobbit popped up suddenly from behind the bar, a look of puzzlement and mild irritation on his face. "Good morning," I said, proffering my shaking hand. "Bill Exley, Observer."

(EXLEY *offers his hand in greeting, and also the tape recorder.* DAVE *takes his hand, and speaks into the recorder.*)

DAVE   (*tentatively*) Dave Dowson, club chairman.

EXLEY   . . . the man replied.

              (EXLEY *flexes his fingers.*)

DAVE   You've come to observe, then, did you say?

EXLEY   That's true. I have come to observe. I have come to observe, for the Observer.

DAVE   (*the light dawns*) Ah! Of course! Welcome, welcome. I was expecting you to come with Nina, you know.

EXLEY   (*blanks* NINA'S *name with an amiable shrug*) Who?

DAVE   Right! Well, have a seat, what can I get you?

EXLEY   Really? It's a bit early in the day, yet, isn't it?

DAVE   (*winks*) Special licence. For the World Cup.

EXLEY   Oh well, in that case, bring me a glass of your least horrible white wine.

DAVE   Right you are, right you are.

              (DAVE *dips behind the bar and makes the drink, energetically.* EXLEY *removes his coat and hangs it up.*)

EXLEY   I was rather under the impression that the joint was going to be jumping.

DAVE   Oh it will be, it will be.

EXLEY   If you build it, they will come, sort of thing?

DAVE   Yeah, something like that. There we are. Nice Hungarian Chardonnay.

EXLEY   Yum yum. You not having one yourself?

DAVE   No, no, I'm fine. (*Holds up a glass of water.*)

EXLEY   Water?

DAVE   Water. So, yeah, I've spent the whole week getting this place ready after the semi last Sunday. The celebrations got a bit out of . . . well, there was a fair bit of water damage.

EXLEY   *Water* damage?

DAVE   Yeah, they set off the sprinklers, that's all, we've got a sprinkler system up there, everything got soaked through, but, you know, what the hell! And if you can't shove toilet paper up your arse and set fire to it in a rugby club then where can you shove toilet paper up your arse and set fire to it? (*Laughs.*)

     (EXLEY *clicks off his tape recorder.*)

DAVE   You won't write that, though, will you?

EXLEY   OK. Cheers.

     (JAKE *comes back in with a dustpan and brush, and begins sweeping up the broken glass from the smashed skylight.*)

DAVE   Cheers . . . See that lad? He'll play for England.

EXLEY   Really?

DAVE   He's the reason we're top of the league this season. The coach'll try to tell you different, probably, oh, it's all down to his training methods, but no. It's Jake.

JAKE   I'm just going to nip home, fetch something, OK Mr Dowson?

DAVE	Right you are.
	(JAKE *exits, meeting* NINA RITCHIE – *the ladies XV captain, a bright woman heading for thirty – in the doorway.*)
NINA	Hallo.
JAKE	Hi. (*Leaves.*)
NINA	Hallo, goodbye.
	(DAVE *bustles over to greet her, as she hangs her coat up.*)
DAVE	Nina, Nina. The chap from the paper is here.
NINA	Oh? (*Cursory wave in* EXLEY'S *direction.*) Where is everyone?
DAVE	Don't you know him? I thought you knew him.
NINA	No, no, never met him before. His boss is a friend of mine, that's who I spoke to.
DAVE	Well, great, that's great. Come and meet him then. Mr Exley?
EXLEY	Bill, please.
DAVE	Bill? This is Nina.
NINA	Hi.
DAVE	She's the captain of our very successful women's fifteen.
EXLEY	Charmed. Women's rugby, eh? How about that.
NINA	(*irritated*) Why is it that whenever a guy hears the phrase "women's rugby", it translates in his head as all-nude lesbian mud wrestling?

EXLEY   Is it not nude, then?

NINA   It's like whenever I hear the phrase "sports
               reporter", it translates in my head as freeloading
               arrogant male bullshit artist.

               (DAVE *is a little alarmed by the spikiness of this
               exchange.*)

DAVE   Ha ha ha. Can I get you something, Nina?

NINA   No, you're all right, thanks. Not on an empty
               stomach. (*To* EXLEY'S *white wine.*) Your body's your
               temple, then, is it?

EXLEY   Pretty much.

NINA   Well, if you'll excuse me, I want to make sure I sit in
               the same place as I sat for the quarter and the semi.
               And there might be a sudden stampede of people
               rushing in . . .

EXLEY   Enjoy.

               (NINA *goes to a table and takes some things from
               her bag: a box of muesli, a bowl, a bottle of milk.
               She has breakfast watching the preliminaries on
               the telly.*)

NINA   You are going to switch the telly on, aren't you,
               David? I'm going to feel a fool sitting here looking
               at the wall.

DAVE   Yeah, in a while. It's only Scooby Doo or something
               at the moment.

NINA   No, there's build up.

DAVE   Christ, look at the time, you're right . . .

               (DAVE *switches on the telly and the projector
               thingy, faffing about with several remotes. Sound
               comes on very loud, and* DAVE *turns it right down.*)

NINA   I want another look at Jim Rosenthal on the big
                screen. I've got a bet on with a friend that his eyes
                are blue.

DAVE   (*muttering*) Where the hell *is* everyone . . . ?

                (MATT HOLDEN – *the first XV coach, in his mid/late
                thirties – is seen through the window heading for
                the doorway, and then he enters like a steam train.
                The audience do not know he is Australian at first,
                ideally. He carries an esky, which he plonks on the
                ground and rushes* DAVE, *tackling him to the
                ground.*)

DAVE   (*from the floor*) Good morning, Matt. Nice to see
                you.

                (MATT *gets up first, and, keeping eye contact with*
                DAVE, *he unzippers his coat to reveal a gleaming
                new green and gold Australian top. It is a bullish
                gesture.*)

MATT   G'day. Where the hell is everyone? It's like a veggie
                barbie in here.

DAVE   Ah, I don't think I've heard that colourful piece of
                Australian slang before.

MATT   I made it up myself on the way over here. Not bad,
                eh?

                (DAVE *grimaces, then notices that* MATT *has
                brought a large esky with him full of cans and
                bottles of Australian beer.*)

DAVE   What've you got there?

MATT   You don't think I'm going to sit here and watch
                Australia win the World Cup – *again* – drinking that
                warm horse piss you Poms call beer, do ya? I
                brought some cold tins and stubbies – plenty to go
                round.

DAVE

I see, well, that's very generous. I hope you don't think that a few beers are going to swing the vote in your favour tomorrow, though.

MATT

Well, I hope *you* don't think that making sandwiches for everybody is going to swing the vote in *your* favour.

DAVE

Of course not.

MATT

You have made sandwiches for everybody, though, haven't you?

DAVE

I'll bring them out at half time.

MATT

Great.

(MATT *brings his esky over to a table, and* DAVE *heads back over to the bar.*)

NINA

Hey, Matt? Catt's out. You know that, don't you?

MATT

(*guilty*) Shit! Who told you?

NINA

They said on the telly just now.

MATT

They said *on the telly*?

NINA

Yeah. Tindall is in.

MATT

(*beat*) *Mike* Catt! *Mike* Catt's out! Right, right . . .

NINA

What did you think I meant?

MATT

Nothing, nothing. I'm just gonna hit the dunny . . .

(*He goes off to the toilet.* NINA *munches more muesli.*)

EXLEY

So, Dave, I believe you have an election coming up tomorrow . . . ?

DAVE

How do you know about that?

EXLEY	A good journalist does his research. And so do I.
DAVE	Oh, I see. Well, yes, there has been a challenge to my chairmanship of the club, um, from the man in the dunny as it happens.
EXLEY	And why is that? Not enough Cointreau injected into the half time oranges . . . ?
DAVE	No, no, it's a difference of opinion, that's all, on the future of the club. See, we have a lease on this ground from the council, and it's a prime spot, right in the middle of the town, which is where we should be, right in the heart of the community. Right Nina?
NINA	I haven't decided yet, David.
DAVE	And he . . . (*Stops himself.*)
	(MATT *comes back in from the dunny, and* JAKE *comes back in the main door at the same moment.*)
MATT	Wilko! There you are!
JAKE	Hi Matt.
MATT	You want a beer?
JAKE	No thanks.
MATT	Go on, I won't tell your mum . . .
	(JAKE *smiles.* MATT *gets him one anyway.* JAKE *comes and sits by* NINA. *He wants to talk to her and is waiting for his chance.*)
MATT	Well, I've been checking the night sky for signs and the news isn't good, fellas.
NINA	What do you mean?
MATT	Moon not blue, complete absence of flying pigs, it's not gonna happen, guys. The natural order of things is asserting itself. We've beat you at tennis, at

cricket, at football, and now we're gonna resume our
rightful place as the kings of rugby union. When are
you lot gonna learn? It's no good inventing games if
you can't bloody play 'em.

(DAVE *has been pacing up and down, looking out
of the window to see if anyone else is coming. he
comes over to* MATT.)

DAVE   Matt, can I have a quick word? It's about Toad.

MATT   Oh, what? All right, what's he done?

DAVE   I'm afraid we've had more complaints about his
              behaviour . . .

MATT   What, a little tiny bit of swearing?

DAVE   Swearing, yes, at the captain of the under 12s last
              week, and at the dad of the under 12s captain who
              asked him to stop swearing. And at the mum of the
              under 12s captain when she complained about him
              breaking the nose of the dad of the under 12s
              captain with his forehead.

MATT   Oh, no, wait a minute. I see what's going on here.
              You reckon if you bring this up before the vote
              Toady'll have to resign from the committee . . .

DAVE   He'll have to.

MATT   . . . and that's one sure fire vote for me down the
              tubes.

DAVE   It's got nothing to do with that.

MATT   Course not, course not. Well, it's not gonna
              work. Toady'll hang on for grim death.

DAVE   I don't see how he can.

MATT   He'll deny it, I'll back him, and the best you
              can do is a hearing next month. Meantime, he's
              voting for me tomorrow, so shove that where

the sun don't shine – not that it shines anywhere in this godforsaken country.

(DAVE *sighs.* JAKE *plucks up the courage to talk to* NINA *while* MATT *is distracted, but he's waited too long.*)

JAKE Nina?

NINA Yes? Hallo, it's Jake, isn't it? I've heard a lot about you. You're the young lad who's carrying the firsts to the county championship single-handed, aren't you?

MATT (*sarcastic*) That's right. It's got absolutely nothing to do with the other fourteen players, or the new fitness regime, or tactics, or coaching.

NINA Yeah, that's what I heard.

(MATT *loses interest in pursuing the conversation.*)

JAKE Actually, everyone's been playing really well this season, not just me.

NINA Oooh, you'll go far. You already talk the talk.

JAKE There's . . . something I want to . . . ask you . . .

(NINA *is distracted by seeing* NIGEL *through the window.*)

NINA Christ on a bike, will you look at that!

(*Then* NIGEL MAITLAND *enters. He is the first team captain – a burly fellow dressed in a nun costume – and he's talking angrily into a mobile phone.*)

NIGEL (*into mobile phone*) Yes, well be like that then, see if I care. (*Hangs up.*) Fucking hormones!

DAVE	Nigel?! What the hell are you doing here?
NIGEL	Charming.
DAVE	I mean, I thought you were there, in Sydney.
NIGEL	I was, I was, but . . . (*Sighs heavily*.) oh . . . I got the call, didn't I? "It's coming, it's coming, I'm on my way to the hospital, you've got to come home now!"
DAVE	Hey! You mean you're a dad? Congratulations! (*Hand outstretched*.)
NIGEL	No, course I'm fucking not. I leapt onto the first flight back to the UK and when I got home a day later she was sitting there, still the size of a house, knitting another two dozen of these ludicrous tiny sock things – "oh, sorry Nigel, it was a false alarm!"
DAVE	When was this?
NIGEL	Wednesday. I called Mattso, did he not say anything?
MATT	Oh, I meant to say, Nigel's back.
DAVE	So is Jo not coming down?
NIGEL	She says it's stupid, grown men dressed as nuns. I told her. Stupid? It's hilarious, that's what it is, mate.
DAVE	So the lads are all nuns today?
NIGEL	That's right. Vikings for the quarters, schoolgirls for the semi, and nuns for the final.
DAVE	Well, take the weight off your wimple. I'll get you a beer.
NIGEL	Yeah, cheers, Daveso. She didn't even want me to come here, you know, this morning. "Oh

don't leave me on my own, I think I just felt a
twinge". (*Sceptical.*) Yeah, that'll be right . . .

DAVE   She might have, though, mightn't she?

NIGEL   What do you mean?

DAVE   Well, it's going to come sometime soon, isn't
            it?

NIGEL   Who cares? I'm starving, actually. What you
            got there, Neenso?

NINA   Muesli. Here . . .

            (*She hands over her bowl.* NIGEL *pours himself
            a helping.*)

NIGEL   Yach, brought to you direct from the birdcage
            floors of Sweden. Hey, Mattso!

            (MATT *slings over a tin of beer.* NIGEL *opens it
            and pours it on his muesli.*)

NINA   I've got milk.

NIGEL   It's all right, I'm lactose intolerant.

NINA   You're allergic to milk?

NIGEL   No, I just don't see why I should tolerate it
            when there's beer.

            (DAVE *comes over with a beer for* NIGEL, *sees
            that he has one from* MATT, *and turns and
            takes it back to the bar.*)

NIGEL   All right there, Wilko? I'm not interrupting
            anything, am I?

JAKE   (*gets up*) No, no, I was just sitting here. I'll go.

NINA   You don't have to. (*To* NIGEL.) What you want
            to do that for?

NIGEL   I didn't want to cramp your style.

NINA   Idiot.

NIGEL   (*Leslie Phillips, seeing* LENA) Ha-llo . . .

               (JAKE *has gone to stand at the back near the
               door, and is consequently the first person to
               meet* LENA POGLIACOMI, *an attractive blonde
               Australian girl, 30-ish, dressed to kill, who
               appears now in the doorway.* JAKE *is
               dumbstruck.*)

LENA   Hallo? Have I come to the right place? I'm
               looking for Matt?

JAKE   Um . . .

LENA   This is the rugby club, right?

JAKE   Um, I think so . . .

               (JAKE *continues to gape.* MATT *spots her and
               bustles over.*)

MATT   Lena, mate. There you are. Dave, this is Lena.

DAVE   Hallo.

LENA   Hi.

MATT   Just a bit of moral support from God's own
               country. Actually I thought you might be able
               to use a bit of help behind the bar . . .

DAVE   Oh, great . . .

MATT   . . . once it starts to get really mad in here.
               (*Looks around, puzzled.*) Although it seems
               pretty quiet just now . . .

DAVE   Oh it'll start filling up any time now. So, you
               worked behind a bar before, Lena?

LENA   No, but I'm Australian so I imagine it'll come
              naturally to me.

MATT   Just remember: if you shape up, there might be
              a job here for you full time, all right, sweetheart?

DAVE   You what?

MATT   You know. Under new management. (*Winks*.)

              (DAVE *snorts contemptuously at the dig.* MATT
              leads LENA *over to his table, where* EXLEY *casts
              an appreciative eye over her from the bar.*)

MATT   Thanks for coming.

LENA   I must be out of my mind.

MATT   It means a lot to me.

LENA   And I'm not working behind the bar. Not with
              these nails.

MATT   Course not, course not. I'll get you a drink,
              what's your poison?

LENA   Rum and Coke.

MATT   Rum and Coke, rum and Coke . . .

              (*Looks through his esky, but it only has beer
              in it, and so he goes over to the bar.* NIGEL
              decides to have a go at flirting with LENA.)

NIGEL   Oh, there it is, look. I was there, you know, the
              Tel-strah stadium.

LENA   (*corrects his pronunciation*) Telstra. Stadium.

NIGEL   (*unfazed, ploughs on*) The worst bit of not
              being there is I can't decide whether I want
              England to win or not.

NINA	What?
NIGEL	I'm not there, am I, so maybe I'd feel better about not being there if we didn't win, and then everyone would feel sorry for the lads who are there, because they'd've gone all that way for nothing. Mind you, if we won, that might be so great that I won't mind about not being there myself . . .
NINA	(*cuts him off*) OK, here we go, then.
DAVE	Here we go, then.
NIGEL	Come on England!
MATT	Come on Aussie!
NIGEL	Come on England!
MATT	Come on Aussie!
NIGEL	Come on England!
MATT	Come on Aussie!
NINA	You're not going to keep this up for the whole game, are you?
	(*Pause. They look at her.*)
NIGEL	Come on England!
MATT	Come on Aussie!
NINA	All right, calm down. I can't take another seventy-nine minutes and forty seconds of that.
	(*Another pause. Then quietly.*)
NIGEL	. . . n'England . . .
MATT	. . . n'Aussie . . .

(*During the above,* EXLEY *moves to join the groups at their tables, trying to capture some atmosphere on tape. Now he clicks his machine off.* MATT *notices, looks puzzled, glances to* DAVE *for enlightenment.*)

DAVE   Oh, this is Mr Exley.

EXLEY   Bill.

DAVE   Matt, the firsts' coach. Mr Exley's a journalist
                for The Observer. Sport section.

MATT   Is that right?

EXLEY   Yeah. I'm supposed to capture the atmosphere
                and the excitement of watching the Final in a
                typical jam-packed English rugby club bar.
                (*Looks around.*) Course, it's early yet . . .

MATT   And when will it be printed this story?

EXLEY   It should be in tomorrow morning, or else it'll
                be a bit out of date, won't it?

MATT   (*light dawning*) Oh right . . . David Dowson
                you are a sly old dog.

DAVE   What?

MATT   Nice little piece in the paper, just in time to
                catch everyone's eye tomorrow, about how the
                club is thriving under your leadership. What a
                shame there's hardly any bugger here.

NINA   So you really know your rugby, then, do you
                Mr Exley?

EXLEY   God no. It's thirty posh blokes fighting, isn't
                it? Or have I missed something? No, I'm a
                football writer, really. Association football, I
                mean. I'm doing Leicester City – Charlton this

afternoon. All the rugby guys are out in
Australia, aren't they?

(NIGEL *grinds his teeth.* DAVE *turns to him.*)

DAVE   So Nigel, what was it like, then?

NIGEL   What was what like?

DAVE   Well, Australia. The World Cup.

NIGEL   You want me to sum up the experience of a
lifetime in a couple of glib sentences?

DAVE   Yes, that'd be nice.

NIGEL   All right.

(EXLEY *gets his tape recorder ready, quickly
intros* NIGEL *before he starts in on his
reminiscences.*)

EXLEY   (*into tape recorder*) Nigel, enormous
transvestite rugger bugger . . . (*Holds machine
out to* NIGEL.)

NIGEL   Well, obviously it was great to see the Taffs
heading home, and the Frogs, and the Sweaties.

LENA   I'm sorry. Sweaties?

NIGEL   Sweaty boll-ocks. Jocks. And I'll tell you what:
they're scared to death of Jonny Wilkinson out
there.

MATT   Naaah, mate . . .

NIGEL   Yeah, all over the papers it's "Is this all you've
got?" like we're a one man team. And the rest
of them they're calling "Dad's Army".

MATT   Well, yeah, that's your whole game plan, isn't
it. A bunch of geriatrics bumbling about trying
to get penalties for the golden boy to convert.

DAVE	It's funny, isn't it, that you are so dismissive of Woodward's tactics when that's exactly how the firsts have been playing all season.
MATT	What do you mean?
DAVE	Carried along by the golden boy's kicking. The lad here.
JAKE	(*embarrassed*) Oh, no . . .
MATT	Well, I'll say this for Woodward: he's got some good ideas. Having a specialist peripheral vision coach, for example, that's great. It means your blokes'll get a great view of the Aussies running past them on the way to the line.
	(NIGEL *suddenly stands up and points at the screen.*)
NIGEL	Nuns!
	(NINA, JAKE *and* MATT *peer closely at screen, too.*)
NINA	Is that them?
NIGEL	Has to be. Hey! Brilliant! Is someone videoing this? For the dinner?
DAVE	Well, I'm taping it in the office.
MATT	I don't know, you know, I don't think it is them.
NIGEL	Course it's them.
JAKE	Well, which one's which then?
NINA	I don't recognise that one for a start.
NIGEL	Which one?

NINA   On the end there. The ginger girl. Australian
                flag painted on her forehead.

NIGEL   There's one way to find out. I'll call them.
                (*Dials on phone.*)

MATT   Oh good luck. Major event like this, the
                airwaves will be jammed solid.

NIGEL   You never know . . .

MATT   I'm telling you. You'll never get a signal
                through.

NIGEL   (*smug*) Ringing . . . Ponce? Ponce-o! Chugger
                chugger chugger! (*Waits for response.*) Hey
                mate! What's it like there? Is it fantastic . . . ?
                (*Turns to others.*) He says it's fantastic. Hey
                we just saw you on the telly! Group of nuns,
                big close up . . . what . . . ? But why not . . . ?
                But we agreed, didn't we? Vikings, then
                schoolgirls, then nuns, it's the classic one-two-
                three . . . Yes . . . yes . . . yes . . . well if it's
                raining I suppose a cagoule is more sensible . . .
                yes, yes, they do hold a lot of water . . . OK . . .
                OK, yeah, we'll be looking out for some blokes
                in cagoules then, fine. Later . . . (*Hangs up
                crossly.*)

NINA   Having a wild time without you, then, are they?

NIGEL   Wankers . . .

                (NIGEL *furiously rips off his nun's habit and
                slings it away, after a bit of a struggle with it.*)

MATT   Look at this, we're all over you. Penalty!

EXLEY   Now, you see, that's the thing that baffles me
                about this game. It's a penalty, but nobody
                ever seems to know why. It's like the ref thinks:
                right they've been banging their heads
                together for long enough, let's have a penalty.

DAVE	There's a punch, there, look.
NINA	Woodman, is it?
DAVE	Silly bugger.
MATT	Ah, now, watch this Mr Exley and you'll see the difference between the two teams. If this was England all the old blokes would have been wheeled back into the home while Jonny Goldenbollocks has a kick at goal. Not us though, watch . . .
EXLEY	Well, he's just kicked it right off the park.
MATT	Going for position, you see, going for tries, that's what rugby's about mate, not some bloody wind up toy booting it over the posts over and over again.
NINA	What's happened there? Too many in the line out? I don't believe it.
MATT	(*cackling with glee*) Oh man, that is an elementary school error. Your boys are bottling it. Hoo hoo!
LENA	Sit down, stop embarrassing me.
EXLEY	Ah, now, look. I may not know much about the game, but even I can see that that is a dreadful kick. It's nowhere near the posts, it's going to hit the corner flag.
MATT	He's not looking for the posts, mate, he's looking for Tuqiri. Here he comes! Go on you big bastard! Lote Tuqiri against Jason Robinson! It's hardly fair, is it? Ye-e-es! Take that, tiny! Bang! Woo hoo!
	(*Australia have scored a try. The English react, appalled.* MATT *embraces* LENA.)
NIGEL	Shit . . .

EXLEY   Now that's called a try, isn't it?

DAVE   That's right.

EXLEY   Well, how did we let that happen, then? Hmm?

NIGEL   Shit . . .

DAVE   How did we let what happen?

EXLEY   How did they get to have that enormous giant
               up against our really little bloke? Shouldn't we
               have a giant as well?

NIGEL   Shit . . .

MATT   Jeez, it's men against boys! It's started, fellas,
               the massacre is officially under way. It's like I
               always say: A good big 'un will beat a good
               little 'un every time.

EXLEY   They don't mess around celebrating, do they?
               Just jog straight back and get on with it.

NIGEL   Shit . . .

DAVE   Come on, we've been behind in nearly every
               game recently. We like being behind, it gets us
               going.

NIGEL   Shit . . .

MATT   Ah . . . he's missed the conversion. Never
               mind, five nil to us. Time for another beer, I
               reckon – although, hang on, if I crack one open
               every time we score I'm gonna be pissed as a
               fart by half time, aren't I. Better pace meself . . .
               Ladies and gentlemen. Normal service is being
               resumed.

NINA   Haven't we beaten you four times in a row?

MATT   I know, I know . . .

NIGEL   You must remember. Last year at Twickenham, 32-31? You went into hiding for a fortnight and came back with a ginger beard?

MATT   Yeah, yeah . . .

NIGEL   And when we won again in the summer you said you'd streak through the shopping arcade.

MATT   And I did.

NIGEL   At four in the morning on Bank Holiday Monday.

MATT   Are you disputing the photographic evidence, mate?

NIGEL   Digital photos taken by the Toad, who happens to be a computer whiz.

DAVE   Amongst other things . . .

MATT   Anyway, look, the point is that this is the big one, and when it comes to the big one, we always pull something out. We've got the edge, up here.

EXLEY   (*scuttles forward with tape recorder*) Ah. Now why is that, do you think?

MATT   Australians just are good at sport. It's genetic. All that good old sturdy convict stock.

EXLEY   Yes, but that's the bit I don't understand. Because what's the one thing all those convicts had in common. Stamina? Speed? Wit? No, it's being caught. They all got caught.

NIGEL   Right.

EXLEY   Whereas our genetic heritage is the ones who managed to get away, or else the policemen who caught your blokes – there always used to be a policeman in the England rugby team, didn't there, in the old days? A great big bloke with huge feet?

MATT   (*looks dangerous for a moment, then grins, winks*) I can't explain it, mate, I just kick back and enjoy it.

               (NIGEL'S *phone rings. It plays "Swing Low Sweet Chariot".* NIGEL *looks at the little screen and sees that it is his wife calling.*)

NIGEL   Oh, what's she want now . . . ? (*Answers phone.*) Yes? . . . I'm at the club, you know where I am . . . Yes, well sit tight, I'm sure it's nothing to worry about . . . It's just nature's way of telling you not to make a fuss . . . Hallo . . . ? Hallo . . . ?

               (*Shakes the phone – it's cut out.*)

NIGEL   Coh! Bloody thing. It's fine when I'm talking to Australia, but half a mile away . . .

DAVE   Maybe it'd work better outside?

               (NIGEL *was going to leave it, but now feels guilty that* DAVE *is concerned, and slowly tears himself away.*)

NIGEL   Yeah, yeah, yeah, all right . . .

               (NIGEL *exits to call his wife back.* MATT *watches him go.* JAKE *takes the opportunity to sidle back over to* NINA *and sit beside her.*)

JAKE   Nina . . . Can I ask you something?

NINA   Sure. What's up?

               (JAKE *leans in closer, and they huddle over so the others can't hear.*)

JAKE   Don't you think it's a bit weird that there's
                only seven of us here, when it was packed out
                for the semi last week?

NINA   (*frowns*) Go on.

JAKE   Well . . . (*Is about to confide his suspicions,
                but suddenly . . .*)

DAVE   Penalty!

NINA   Penalty? To us? Yes!

JAKE   Where?

DAVE   Fifty yards out, bang in the middle.

MATT   Ah, run it, you cowards.

                (MATT *puts his head in his hands and doesn't
                see* JAKE *going out at a trot. After a moment*
                MATT *heads for the bar in disgust, indicating
                slyly to* LENA *that she should follow him. She
                does, taking her own sweet time . . .*)

EXLEY   See this is what I'm talking about. They were
                all just scrabbling about on the ground, and
                now it's a penalty. What for?

DAVE   Stamping.

MATT   (*calls*) Offside.

NINA   No, he's gone over the top, there . . .

EXLEY   See, you don't know, do you? None of you
                knows.

                (*At the bar,* MATT *and* LENA *sotto voce. he
                talking about* NIGEL, *she thinking he's talking
                about* JAKE.)

MATT   So, you clocked him, right? He just went
                outside.

LENA   (*surprised*) Really? That one?

MATT   What's up?

LENA   Nothing. I suppose I thought he'd be older.
                From the way you were talking about him.

MATT   So are we on? You did say as long as he didn't
                look like a warthog . . . ?

LENA   Oh yes, I'd say we're on.

                (*In the centre of the room,* DAVE, EXLEY *and*
                NINA *watch the real Jonny Wilkinson line up
                his kick, absorbed, nervous, willing him to
                succeed. Except* EXLEY, *who doesn't seem to
                care.*)

NINA   Come on Jonny Wilko . . . !

                (*Lights out.*)

                            Scene Three

In the blackout, we hear a snatch of commentary.

COMMENTATOR   "Jonny Wilkinson, forty yards out, smack in
                front – it should be all about whether he's got
                the length . . ."

                (*Lights up on the field.* JAKE *is out on the
                pitch, ready to take his first kick of the match.
                Breathless, in a bit of a hurry. Crouches to put
                the ball on its little support.*)

JAKE   It was Mr Dowson's idea making Jonny
                Wilkinson my role model. I kick like Jonny,
                same exact routine. Imagine kicking to a girl in
                the crowd – I got that from him, from a
                documentary. (*Drifts.*) The girl from the fitness
                centre. What's she doing here . . . ? Focus . . .
                (*Snaps out of it – stands up.*) I read Jonny's

book, and found I was starting to think like him. The lads have even started calling me Wilko.

(*Paces backwards, clasps hands together a la Jonny Wilko.*)

JAKE   Now, whenever England are playing, I come down to the club and match Jonny's kicking. He has a penalty fifty yards out, I take a penalty fifty yards out as well. Just a silly superstition. (*Kicks, watches it go. It is a long one, and good.*) Nailed it. (*Drifts again.*) Lena, her name is . . .

(*Back to in the room.*)

Scene Four

As soon as the lights go back up, all Englanders cheer real Jonny Wilkinson's successful kick. MATT *curses under his breath. He and* LENA *have finished their secret chat, and she now goes to the changing room to freshen up.*

DAVE   Yes! Jonny Wilko!

MATT   One man team.

NINA   Yes, but what a man. Hey, where did Jake go? I was just talking to him.

DAVE   He's out there. Whenever Jonny takes a kick, Jake goes out there and takes the same kick, near as he can. It's like a superstition, that's all. Kids! (*Beat, then touches wood.*)

(NIGEL *comes in from car park – he has missed seeing the penalty.*)

NIGEL   What happened? What was that cheer?

DAVE   Penalty, Jonny Wilkinson. Sweet as the proverbial nut.

NIGEL   Excellent. So that's what . . . ? Five-three?

DAVE   Yep.

NIGEL   Where's the score? Isn't the score supposed to
               be in the top corner?

DAVE   Oh, yeah, this new screen, it's in the wrong, I
               don't know, proportion, or something, so
               there's a strip missing at the top and the
               bottom.

NIGEL   Oh.

DAVE   If you get up on a step ladder you can see the
               score projected very faintly onto the wall up
               there, look.

NIGEL   Oh.

NINA   So is everything all right?

NIGEL   No it's not. You have to get on a stepladder to
               see the chuffing score, does that sound all
               right to you?

NINA   The phone call, I meant.

NIGEL   Oh she's fine, she's fine. She was having some
               sort of . . . discomfort, but then it just sort of
               went away again. Nothing to worry about, I'm
               sure.

NINA   Do you know what it's going to be yet? Boy or
               a girl?

NIGEL   What do I care? A baby. It's going to be a
               baby. It's the end of my travelling abroad to
               watch England, that's what it is. It's the end of
               my freedom to live my life. They can see that,
               you know, in the scan they do, where they
               squirt grease all over her great bloated belly
               and show her insides on the gogglebox.

NINA	Lovely, you make it sound really beautiful.
NIGEL	And the doctor goes, "Look, see, if I just tilt it round this way . . . ah yes, there it is, the end of your life as you know and love it. Aaaaah!"
MATT	Just a couple of tips about the actual birth, mate. When the baby's born, remember to wait till the baby is completely out from between your wife's legs before you handle it, OK, and then whatever you do don't go driving over the top and getting offside.
NIGEL	Thanks, Mattso.
MATT	Benefit of my experience.
DAVE	I didn't know you had kids, Matt.
MATT	I used to drive a cab.
EXLEY	Dave, England are off the mark, as I understand it. How about a drink?
DAVE	No, that's all right, thanks.
MATT	Dave was quite seriously ill last year, weren't you Dave? If you ask me, it's the strain of running this club. It's ruined your health. You should step aside – for your own good. Let a younger, fitter, better man take over.
DAVE	I am fine. I just would rather not drink alcohol at nine o'clock in the morning. OK?
	(DAVE *strides away, leaving* EXLEY *and* MATT *together.* EXLEY *decides to have a go at interviewing* MATT.)
EXLEY	So Matt . . . (*Into tape machine.*) Squashy face, pushing forty . . . you're the first team coach, right?

MATT	Yep.
EXLEY	And what do you do in the real world?
MATT	I am the manager of a sports . . .
NIGEL	(*butts in*) Deputy manager.
MATT	Right, deputy manager of a sports and fitness centre.
EXLEY	Righto.
NIGEL	Very handy for the tanning salon and the nail bar, eh, Mattso?
MATT	I'm more on the weights and personal training side of the operation.
NIGEL	Yes, and you get a great staff discount on a bikini wax.
EXLEY	Dave was telling me that the team is doing well this season.
MATT	Well, we're top of the league. Can't get much better than that.
EXLEY	And it's all thanks to young Jake, he tells me.
MATT	Yeah, he would say that, wouldn't he.
EXLEY	Is that not the case, then?
MATT	Oh, the kid's playing well enough, but Dave would have you believe we're a one man band, because Jake is like Dave's project.
EXLEY	His project?
MATT	Well, he found him, didn't he, God knows where, and brought him down to the club. First week they gave him a go in the fifths, and within a month he was the regular kicker for the

first fifteen. Put a couple of noses out of joint, that did, I can tell you.

(*Suddenly there's some excitement on screen.*)

NIGEL   Look at this! It's a try, it's a try, got to be . . . !

NIGEL/NINA/   (*in agony*) Aughhhh!
DAVE

MATT   He's knocked it on, can you believe it? Ha ha ha!

DAVE   Who was that?

NINA   Ben Kay.

NIGEL   Unbelievable. Fucking unbelievable.

MATT   I'm tellin' yer. This is where the game's won, mate. Up here.

                 (MATT *taps his brainbox.* NIGEL's *phone rings again.*)

NIGEL   Tchah! Yes, what now . . . ? Well, correct me if I'm wrong, but if the pain is coming and going then all you have to do is wait until it goes, or am I being very stupid . . . ? Hallo . . . ?

                 (*Phone has cut off.* NIGEL *looks at it.*)

NIGEL   Unbe-*lieve*-able!

NINA   Well, hadn't you better call her back?

NIGEL   Yes, yes, all right, I'm going . . . Coh . . . !

                 (NIGEL *stomps out to car park.*)

DAVE   Ah, now this is better, this is a great drive . . .

                 (*A penalty is given.*)

NINA   Yes! That'll be right on the twenty-two.

MATT   No! What is going on here?

EXLEY   I presume it's a penalty, is it? For arse-biting or
                handling the ball by the pointy ends or
                something?

MATT   Yes that's right, it's another fucking penalty,
                and *obviously* they're going to kick it.

                (MATT *slumps in his chair, dejected.* DAVE *is
                going to the door to shout* JAKE.)

DAVE   (*remembers*) Oooh, Jake! (*Dashes over to the
                door, calls.*) Jake?! Penalty to England. Forty
                yards out, smack in front.

NINA   Yes, come on then Jonny Wilko. Let's have
                another.

                (*Lights out.*)

Scene Five

In the blackout, we hear a snatch of commentary.

COMMENTATOR   "Jonny Wilkinson now has the chance to put
                England into the lead . . ."

                (*Lights up on* JAKE, *on the field. He finds the
                right place, and begins his preparation.*)

JAKE   Lena. I saw her, not long ago. I went to the
                fitness centre with Matt to help him unload his
                van. Sunbeds, it was. Matt said it was a two
                man job, but I was the only one available so
                he'd have to make do with one and a half. She
                was there. And ever since I've been thinking
                about her. Not in a psycho way, just . . .
                thinking about her, you know. What's she
                doing here? Maybe she's with Matt . . . Come
                on, now, concentrate! It's the World Cup final,
                for Christ's sake!

(*Back step, back step, back step, clasp hands, look up, exhale.*)

JAKE   A silly superstition, that's all this was. The thing is, though . . . When I score, Jonny scores. When I miss, Jonny misses. Just a coincidence, that's what I thought at first . . . Except that if I get this one, it'll be seventy-one coincidences in a row.

(LENA *enters suddenly just as* JAKE *is about to start his run up to kick.*)

LENA   Hi.

(JAKE, *taken by surprise, false starts, aborts, air kicks.*)

JAKE   Fuck . . . ! Oh, hi.

(LENA *holds out her hand to shake hands, and when* JAKE *takes it she keeps hold of his.*)

LENA   Have we met before? Only you seemed to recognise me earlier on . . . ?

JAKE   We haven't exactly met, no. I've seen you at the fitness centre in town.

LENA   That's right, you might've. So the pressure's getting to you, then.

JAKE   What?

LENA   You're not watching the game. I thought maybe it was all too much.

JAKE   Oh yeah, yeah. Um, I was just about to . . .

LENA   Oh yes, of course, go ahead . . .

(*She lets go of his hand, and he quickly gets into position.*)

LENA   (*just as he steadies himself*) Don't mind me . . .

                (JAKE *composes himself once more, and then . . .*)

LENA   Pretend I'm not here . . .

                (JAKE *smiles, polite but wretchedly agitated now.*)

JAKE   Please.

                (LENA *mimes zipping her mouth shut. She stands perfectly still.* JAKE'S *eyes flick over to her a couple of times. He begins to run up, and her phone goes off.*)

JAKE   Shit . . . !

                (*He goes through with the kick, thrown, and is not too confident. He and* LENA *watch the flight of the ball,* JAKE *exhales with relief.* LENA *takes out her phone.*)

LENA   Oooh! Just, well done. Lucky it wasn't too far. (*Clicks phone on.*) Hallo . . . ? Yes I am, I am, I'll call you later, OK.

                (*She switches phone off.* JAKE *listens, and we hear the others over in the bar cheering as Wilkinson's penalty goes over.*)

JAKE   (*to himself*) Seventy-two.

LENA   So you're not wearing a wedding ring, I see.

JAKE   What would I want to do that for?

LENA   Quite right, you don't want to put the girls off, do you?

JAKE   Girls? What girls?

LENA   That's a nice shirt, it's kind of an old style one, isn't it?

JAKE   Er, yeah, it is actually.

              (LENA *moves closer, and she takes the*
              opportunity to stroke the material of his shirt.)

LENA   I like it, they should go back to them, don't you
              think? Mind you, those new kits are quite
              revealing, aren't they? Don't leave much to the
              imagination. What you see is what you get,
              kind of thing.

JAKE   You like rugby, do you?

LENA   Rugby? No, not much. Rugby players, though,
              that's a different story. Course you have to
              catch 'em young, because after a while they all
              look like they've been kicked by a horse.

              (JAKE *laughs.*)

LENA   Someone like Jonny Wilkinson, say, I reckon I
              could go for him.

JAKE   What? You're Australian, aren't you, how can
              you say that?

LENA   Yeah, and George Clooney's American, and
              there's nothing in my passport says I have to
              kick him out of bed either.

JAKE   Sorry. Stupid.

LENA   Jonny Wilkinson. He's quiet, intense, I could
              go for that. I could go for that in a big way.

JAKE   (*beat*) I've modelled myself on Jonny
              Wilkinson.

LENA   Really. That's interesting. And what's Jonny
              Wilkinson's philosophy of life then?

JAKE   Um . . . well, you get out what you put in.

(LENA *licks her lips.* JAKE *raises his eyebrows.*)

(*Lights out. A passage of time occurs here in the blackout, which can be helped by a bit of commentary.*)

COMMENTATOR   (*over crowd cheering*) "That's three out of three for Jonny Wilkinson now . . ."

Scene Six

In the bar. NIGEL *comes hurrying back in from the car park. Jumps up and down trying to see the score above the top edge of the screen.*

NIGEL   Score?

NINA   Nine-five England.

NIGEL   What? I missed another one?

NINA   Two penalties – there he is, look. Jonny Wilkinson. Sighs dreamily. Aaaaaahh . . .

EXLEY   So, that answers that question then.

NINA   Which question's that, Mr Exley?

EXLEY   The one about whether women find Jonny Wilkinson attractive.

NIGEL   I wouldn't have thought he was your type.

NINA   I didn't know I had a type.

NIGEL   I just meant . . . that Jonny Wilkinson strikes me as a bit . . . bland.

NINA   Maybe bland is what I like. Maybe I drink decaffeinated coffee and wear beige chinos. Anyway, I'm not daydreaming about *chatting* to him, am I.

(MATT *giggles at* NIGEL'S *expense and goes out to the dunny again.* NIGEL *takes revenge by shaking up the cans of beer in the esky through the next bit.*)

NIGEL   Hey. Who's the totty with Mattso, then, anyone know?

NINA   Your wife's about to have a baby

NIGEL   I *know* . . .

NINA   Listen, if it's totty you want, we've got a home game next week.

NIGEL   What? Ogle a bunch of female rugby players? I'm not that desperate.

NINA   (*gives him a quizzical look*) Oh, really? Yes, I'm sure you could come into the showers with all of us after a game without embarrassing yourself.

NIGEL   Not a problem.

NINA   Fifteen ladies, all of us wet and soapy. And giggling.

NIGEL   Cackling, more like.

NINA   I bet you couldn't. You'd be a human sundial inside a minute. I bet you twenty quid.

NIGEL   Leave me alone.

EXLEY   Wouldn't bother me, I could do it. When's your next match?

NINA   What are you saying, Mr Exley? You don't fancy me?

EXLEY   It's not that, believe me, it's just that I've been clinically impotent for the last three years, so it'd be money for old rope.

(NINA *looks at him for a moment, then gets up to go.* NIGEL *meanwhile grabs a beer bottle and turns his back to the audience.*)

NINA   The showers are open to club members only.

EXLEY   So to speak . . .

(NINA *goes over to talk to* DAVE, *leaving* EXLEY *and* NIGEL *alone.*)

NIGEL   Nice one, mate.

(NIGEL *turns around and places the beer bottle, into which he has quickly relieved himself, on the table next to where* MATT *has been sitting.*)

NINA   Cheer up, David. We're winning, you know, nine-five.

DAVE   I know, yes.

NINA   Lot on your mind?

DAVE   Eh? Oh, tomorrow you mean. Actually I was thinking about my father. We used to watch all the matches together, all the England matches. He used to get tickets for Twickenham, either from work or from the ballot here, and we'd always go, right from the early seventies. Wales were the team, in those days, of course, Barry John, Phil Bennett, Gareth Edwards . . . I can remember watching Dad, too, as a player. Like a bull, he was, great shoulders on him.

NINA   Is he . . . I mean, is he still . . . with us?

DAVE   Well, arguably. Parkinsons. (*Suddenly spots something on screen.*) Come on . . . !

NINA   Oh dear.

DAVE   He's had it for years, but it's quite advanced
            now. He's in a full time care home, the Victoria,
            just behind the big Asda, you know?

NINA   Not really.

DAVE   Two years now. I see him every day. It
            wouldn't be quite so bad, I don't think – I
            mean, it would still be bad, but just not quite
            so bad – if I could still talk to him, but . . . Last
            week I went in there and he was convinced that
            he had a game about to start, that he was going
            to play, and he was desperate for me to help
            him get his boots on, can you believe it, and I . . .

            (DAVE *sighs, smiles.* NINA *says nothing.* NIGEL'S
            phone goes again – "Swing Low Sweet
            Chariot".)

NIGEL   (*answers crossly*) Hallo . . . ! (*No signal.*) Shit . . . !

            (NIGEL *goes out of the room again looking at
            his phone malevolently.*)

DAVE   I should be watching this with him, really,
            that's what I was thinking, but he'd as likely
            fall asleep, or want to switch over to cartoons.
            I'll take the tape over later. This was always
            our thing, you see, father and son.

NINA   You've no children yourself, have you?

DAVE   No, no, no. We tried, of course, but . . . One of
            those things. (*Then on the screen he sees . . .*)
            Oh that is a great drive on . . .

            (*Their conversation ends, they watch the
            screen intently.* EXLEY *leans over to talk to*
            MATT.)

EXLEY   Matt? Can I get a couple of words?

MATT   What, for your article, is it?

EXLEY   How do you think it's going?

MATT   I'm confident. Ooooh! (*Reacting to something on screen. He takes a big swig from his beer bottle, looks at it quizzically, shrugs, carries on.*) England, you see, they always fall at the final hurdle.

EXLEY   What about tomorrow? Think you're going to win that one?

MATT   Ah, well, that's a difficult one to call, but look what I'm up against. This is the World Cup final, should be a big earner for a club like this, this bar should be packed out, and how many of us are there? (*Counts heads.*) Four. I reckon it looks bad.

EXLEY   (*leans in, conspiratorial*) Still, let me ask you this. Supposing I could tell you something that would take your rival out of the running.

MATT   Like what?

EXLEY   Just supposing.

               (MATT *looks at* EXLEY *for a moment, then gets to his feet.*)

MATT   The changing rooms? Yeah, they're through here, mate, I'll show you.

               (EXLEY *gets up and follows him towards the changing room.* DAVE *comes over, anxious.*)

DAVE   Where are you going?

MATT   Mr Exley wanted a quick look at our facilities, I'm just showing him.

DAVE   I can do that, you watch the game.

MATT   No, no, you're all right, I don't mind. (*To* EXLEY.) Through here . . .

(DAVE *doesn't like this, but he has to lump it.*
MATT *and* EXLEY *go through to changing
rooms,* MATT *slamming the door in* DAVE'S
face.)

Scene Seven

In changing room – benches, pegs, a couple of lockers.

MATT *checks that* DAVE *isn't listening to them, then eagerly
turns to* EXLEY, *who has sat down on a bench.*

MATT   So you got something on Dave? What is it?
              Pictures? Compromising pictures? Is it?

EXLEY   Let's say it's something that might persuade
              him to pull out of the election altogether.

MATT   It's animals, isn't it? I knew it, I fuckin' knew it.
              Fuckin' English, they fuckin' love their animals.

EXLEY   No, now look, slow down. Supposing – just
              supposing – I had something like that, what
              would it be worth. To you?

MATT   You asking me for money?

EXLEY   Ting! The light dawns.

MATT   What makes you think I'd have money for
              something like that?

EXLEY   Oh, just that I did a little bit of digging, before
              I came. For the article, you know. I read that
              there is some serious interest in relocating the
              club out beyond the ring road and developing
              the site into houses or supermarkets or both.

MATT   Oh, you read that, did you?

EXLEY   And I thought to myself: interest like that
              doesn't leave things to chance. David would

clearly rather be boiled in oil than allow the
club to be bulldozed, so I reckon you're their
man. They must be slipping you a hefty wedge
to swing the committee behind a move. Bung
me some of that and I can help you make it
happen.

(MATT *frowns, wonders if he is being accused,
and is silent for a moment.*)

MATT   I don't know what you're talking about.

EXLEY   (*shrugs*) OK.

(EXLEY *gets up and goes back into the bar.*
MATT *follows, thoughtful.*)

Scene Eight

Back in the bar. EXLEY *goes back to his seat.* MATT *strolls
round, as if continuing their conversation.*

NIGEL   Whew! Tindall just threw Gregan into touch,
              you see that?

MATT   You see, what you've got to remember, Mr
              Exley, is that rugby is a rough game. We've all
              had bad injuries at one time or another. Dave?

DAVE   Um . . . knee, hip, dislocated shoulder.

MATT   I've broken both legs.

EXLEY   Well that's just carelessness.

MATT   Nina, I dare say you've fractured an eyelash or
              two in your time?

NINA   I tell you, you get your tit tweaked in the scrum
              and you know about it, mate.

MATT   Nigel's is the worst, though. Tell him.

NIGEL   About?

MATT   Your jaw mate. Nigel, right, took a kick in the
            face, couple of years back, fractured his jaw all
            over the place. The bone was just splintered.
            The doctors fixed it, though, it's an amazing
            story, by grafting a small piece of dog bone in
            there.

EXLEY   Dog bone?

MATT   Bone from a dog.

EXLEY   You're joking.

MATT   No, show him Nige.

NIGEL   Just here. There's hardly even a scar any more,
            but you can feel it, here, touch it . . .

            (EXLEY, *fascinated and appalled, tentatively
            reaches out to stroke* NIGEL'S *jaw. Suddenly*
            NIGEL *makes a noise like a dog and makes to
            bite* EXLEY'S *hand.*)

NIGEL   Rowf!

EXLEY   Aaaargh!

            (*All laugh, and* EXLEY *goes quiet.* NIGEL'S
            phone rings.)

NIGEL   Oh for crying out loud . . . (*Answers it.*) I'll call
            you at half time . . . (*To* DAVE.) How long till
            half time, now?

DAVE   Couple of minutes, maybe.

NIGEL   I said I'll call you at . . . Oh, God damn this
            bloody contraption . . .

            (NIGEL *has been cut off. He gets up, goes
            towards the door.*)

DAVE   Aren't you going to wait till half time?

NIGEL   No, she didn't hear me say that. I'm going to
            call her back now to tell her that I'll call her at
            half time. She's hysterical, she says she's spilt
            some water, or something . . . (*To screen.*)
            Don't score, you bastards!

            (NIGEL *heads out to the car park. As soon as
            he has gone . . .*)

DAVE   Here's Dallaglio, this looks good . . .

MATT   Jump on him, you fuckers . . .

DAVE   That's well done. Jonny Wilkinson now . . .

MATT   Flatten him, you arseholes . . .

NINA   Outside! Go outside!

DAVE   Jason Robinson . . . Billy Whizz!

MATT   Kill him, you soft steaming piles of . . .

NINA   Yes-s-s!

DAVE   (*applauding*) That is a great try!

NINA   Fantastic!

DAVE   Come on, Matt, you've got to admit. That was
            sheer class. As a rugby man, you have to stand
            and applaud. Come on now. You know you
            want to.

MATT   Shite . . . !

EXLEY   Hey, wasn't that the little bloke you were
            taking the piss out of earlier?

            (MATT *gives him a dangerous look. Lights out.*)

Scene Nine

On the pitch. LENA *is still flirting with* JAKE. JAKE *has heard the cheer, and has one ear cocked towards the pavilion as he explains his kicking technique to her.*

JAKE   What Jonny Wilkinson does is he visualises
            kicking the ball through the posts, and on past
            the posts to a specific person in the crowd,
            maybe a girl he likes the look of. And now I
            haven't got a crowd, here, so I have to imagine
            that part, and . . . since I saw you the other
            week at the fitness centre, I've been imagining
            kicking the ball to you.

LENA   Really. Well, I'll tell you. I've heard some lines
            in my time.

JAKE   Sorry. Embarrassing.

            (DAVE *calls from the doorway of the bar, we
            hear him distant.*)

DAVE   (*off*) Try to England, Robinson, left hand
            corner, right by the flag . . . !

JAKE   Yes! (*Clenches his fist and quickly begins his
            preparation to take the conversion.*)

LENA   It's not embarrassing, no. It's rather sweet,
            actually, if you want to know the truth.

            (JAKE *paces out the run up backwards, which
            brings him right up to where* LENA *is now
            standing. He does the trademark Jonny
            Wilinson stoop, hands together in front.*)

LENA   So what you're saying is: I'm kind of your . . .
            inspiration, then.

            (*Standing beside him she runs her finger
            slowly down his back. Under her flirty
            scrutiny* JAKE *begins to feel uncomfortable.*

His hands move down slowly to cover his groin.)

JAKE   Are you going back inside?

LENA   In a minute. Aren't you going to have a kick?

JAKE   Um . . . yeah . . . OK . . .

            (*Blackout.*)

Scene Ten

Begins with DAVE *and* NINA'S *disappointment at that Jonny Wilkinson conversion, which is a cock-up, so to speak.*

DAVE   Oh, you know what, that's a shocking kick!

NINA   Never mind, never mind.

DAVE   He looked really uncomfortable in his run up, then, didn't you think?

NINA   There it is. Half time. Phew. So far so good, eh?

            (NIGEL *comes back in,* MATT, EXLEY, DAVE *all head to the bar.*)

NIGEL   Half time? Nine-five. Excellent.

NINA   Fourteen-five, you mean.

NIGEL   What? No! I mean . . . yes! (*Bewildered about how to feel momentarily.*)

NINA   She's got timing, your wife, I'll say that for her.

            (NIGEL *charges out again to call his wife.* JAKE *comes in from the field, and goes over to* DAVE.)

JAKE   Mr Dowson? Er, Dave, I mean. Are the showers on?

DAVE   Should be, son, just let 'em run for a minute.

(JAKE *crosses to changing room, and is accosted by* NINA *on the way.*)

NINA   Jake? What was it you wanted to talk to me about?

(JAKE *looks around shiftily, and beckons her into the changing rooms with him, as* LENA *strolls into the bar from outside.*)

Scene Eleven

In changing rooms. NINA *and* JAKE *come through from the bar.* JAKE *absent-mindedly takes off his top.*

JAKE   Now look. Are you voting for Dave or for Matt?

NINA   I don't know yet. Why, are you going to buy my vote with sexual favours?

JAKE   No, no. Sorry . . .

(*Holds his shirt in front of himself.*)

NINA   It's all right, I've seen a man's chest before. So what's the problem?

JAKE   It's this. I got this e-mail a couple of days ago.

(JAKE *takes out a piece of paper and gives it to* NINA, *who glances at it.*)

NINA   It says that the club bar will not be open this morning for screening the final, owing to water damage caused by the sprinklers last week.

JAKE   And it looks like it's gone to everyone, so no wonder hardly anyone has turned up.

NINA   Well, I didn't get this.

JAKE   Oh. Didn't you?

NINA   And it's signed David Dowson, which doesn't
            make any sense at all.

JAKE   Well . . .

NINA   What?

JAKE   You know he's not been himself. He was in
            hospital a while back. I don't know what for.
            He didn't want anyone to know. Maybe this is
            . . . I don't know, maybe he's having a sort of
            breakdown or something.

NINA   (*dubious*) Do you think?

JAKE   Dunno . . .

NINA   What if . . . someone else sent this, faked it, to
            make David look bad? Is that possible? That
            would explain why I didn't get it, 'cos I'm an
            undecided, aren't I. But Matt? Matt's not . . .
            clever enough to do that, is he?

JAKE   No, but Toad is.

NINA   Toad?

JAKE   Yeah. Toad works in IT. He designs security
            systems for internal networks, or something.

NINA   Toad? He can't even use cutlery, are you
            telling me he's some sort of uber nerd?
            (*Grimaces thoughtfully.*) I'll have to have a
            think about this. OK?

JAKE   Yeah.

            (NINA *gets up and goes back into the bar.*
            Meanwhile JAKE *continues undressing in the*
            changing room. He goes off into the wings,
            and comes back with a towel wrapped round
            his waist, then goes round into the showers,
            and we hear showers start up. His hand
            appears round the corner and hangs the towel

*up on the nearest peg – all through
"gloating" bit in the bar.*)

Scene Twelve

DAVE, EXLEY *and* MATT *are over by the bar.* LENA *has come in
after* JAKE, *and now that she sees* NINA *coming out of the
changing rooms she is bracing herself to go in there herself.*
NINA *sits down by herself and looks at the e-mail again, trying
to make sense of things.*

DAVE   I won't know what to do if we win, you know. If
            we win. (*Touches wood.*)

EXLEY   Well, no, we're English, we just haven't got
            any experience, have we.

MATT   I can give you a few pointers if you like.

DAVE   Oh, I think a firm handshake and a smile of
            quiet satisfaction should fit the bill.

MATT   What? No mate, it's very important to gloat,
            get some good gloating in. You've always got
            to think about the next time, you see. You
            don't want to be watching the other guy
            gloating, and thinking to yourself, "Oh, I wish
            I'd done a bit more gloating when we won".
            Rub his nose in it.

DAVE   Your nose, you mean?

MATT   I won't mind, mate. Come on, look. England
            have won, I'm here. Show me what you're
            gonna do, come on.

DAVE   Oh, er . . . (*Offers his hand.*) Um, really bad luck
            . . . um . . . mate . . . still, never mind, only a
            game, eh? And so on . . . ? You want a drink?

MATT   No! No, no no! That's crap city, that is. How
            am I gonna have any respect for you after that,
            eh? Crush me, grind me into the dirt, come on.

DAVE   No, you're all right . . .

MATT   This is why England never win anything.
                Embarrassment. All right, if Australia win –
                what am I talking about, when Australia win –
                this is what you're getting, OK . . . (*Very loud.*)
                Yaaaargh! Take that, you bludgers! You soft as
                shite mummy's boys! You threw it away again,
                you unbelievable wankers, you
                tossaaaarrrrrrrrrrrgh! (*Right in* DAVE'S *face.*)

DAVE   Well. Thanks for the tip.

                (NIGEL *enters and goes over to* NINA. LENA
                catches MATT'S *eye, and nods towards the
                changing rooms. For* MATT *this is a nod
                towards* NIGEL, *and he gives her a thumbs up
                in agreement. Through next bit,* LENA *goes,
                shiftily, into the changing rooms looking for*
                JAKE. *She sees he is not there, sees his clothes
                on peg, hears the shower is running, has a
                quick glance round the corner to check, then
                walks through the changing room and off into
                the wings.*)

NIGEL   I was surprised to see you here.

NINA   (*folds the e-mail away*) That's right, because
                I'm not really interested in rugby at all, am I?

NIGEL   You know what I mean.

NINA   Well, I was rather expecting you to be in
                Australia for the duration.

NIGEL   Yes, well, now that I'm back, I thought we'd
                agreed that it would just be too awkward for
                both of us to stay members here, and that one
                of us should leave.

NINA   There's the door, Nigel.

NIGEL   I'm the first fifteen captain.

NINA   So?

NIGEL   So it's not really fair on the rest of the lads if I
            just walk out on them. They depend on me.

NINA   Except for the last month when you walked out
            on them to go to Australia.

NIGEL   Oh, come on, Daveso managed to rearrange
            most of the fixtures, and anyway, half the lads
            were out there with me.

NINA   Well I'm the captain of the ladies team, aren't
            I? So it would hardly be fair if I walked out on
            them in the middle of the season.

NIGEL   (*little snort*) Ladies team . . .

NINA   Yes, the ladies team, which is the only team in
            the history of this club to have ever won a
            trophy of any kind.

NIGEL   Ladies trophy . . .

NINA   The County Cup, thank you very much. Which
            ought to be on show here in the clubhouse
            except we haven't got a trophy cabinet. I
            suppose a whole cabinet would be a bit
            excessive, given the conspicuous lack of
            success of the five men's teams over the
            years . . .

NIGEL   David put your team photo up, didn't he?

NINA   Eventually, and where has he put it? Stuck
            behind the big screen, which is down whenever
            the bloody bar is open.

NIGEL   Look. I don't want to talk about that now.

NINA   He tolerates a ladies team so the club qualifies
            for lottery money.

NIGEL   I thought we agreed, that's the point I was
             making. I thought we agreed that it would be
             for the best . . .

NINA   For me to give up the sport that I love just
             because you accidentally got your wife
             pregnant and decided you had to go running
             back to her.

NIGEL   You'd find another team.

NINA   I don't want another team. I started this one,
             it's mine. I started it from scratch. You could
             find another team. You could find another wife.

             (*A moment's glaring silence between them.*)

EXLEY   (*squinting at screen*) You know, that Jim
             Rosenthal has brown eyes . . . in there
             somewhere . . .

DAVE   I reckon people have got up, watched the first
             half at home, and now there'll be a mad dash to
             get here, and the place will start filling up any
             minute, you'll see.

MATT   Tossaaaargh! (DAVE *looks back at him, he
             raises his beer in salute.*) Practising . . .

             (*Now, in the changing room,* LENA *appears
             from wings with just a towel round her, walks
             back through the changing room, and follows*
             JAKE *round into the showers. Then her hand
             reaches back round and hangs towel up on a
             peg.*)

             Blackout. End of Act One.

ACT TWO

Scene One

In the bar. NIGEL, DAVE, NINA, EXLEY *and* MATT *are watching the game seated at the tables.* JAKE *sits alone by the bar. There are some plates of sandwiches.*

It is midway through the second half of the match. Australia have pulled back to 14-8, so the English are a little apprehensive – England not playing well at the moment – while MATT *is absorbed, energised. They watch in silence for a while. Crowd noise, commentary, which fades down once dialogue starts.*

COMMENTATOR   (*voice over*) "Australia back in touch now, England 14 Australia 8, just the one score in it now . . ."

               (*After a moment or two* LENA *comes out of the changing room. She is now wearing* JAKE'S *shirt – ie,* DAVE'S *old England Possible shirt – which* DAVE *doesn't clock as she crosses the room to join* JAKE *at the bar. He sees her though, and assumes she wants serving.*)

DAVE   Lena, what can I get you?

JAKE   It's OK, Mr . . . Dave, I've got it.

DAVE   OK.

               (JAKE *scuttles round the bar to get* LENA *a drink, and* DAVE, *happy to leave him to it, goes back to watching the game.*)

EXLEY   (*into tape recorder, composing*) If only that long ago games teacher had had the good sense to shout out, "Webb Ellis?! Deliberate handball – you're off!", then none of us would have been here this morning.

DAVE   Are you really not getting just the tiniest bit
                interested in this, Mr Exley? It's the World Cup
                final, and England are still winning, you know.

EXLEY   It's a World Cup final, and they'll find a way to
                mess it up, don't you worry.

                (NINA *and* NIGEL *both wince at a tackle on-screen.*)

MATT   Sterling Mortlock is a monster. He's a monster.

DAVE   Right . . . Who needs a drink?

NIGEL   Good man, Daveso. Lager beer for me.

DAVE   Right you are . . .

                (MATT *reaches into his esky and slings a can
                of lager across, which* NIGEL *catches.* DAVE *is
                put out.*)

NIGEL   Cheers, coach.

DAVE   Nina?

NINA   Um, yeah, I'll have a b—

                (MATT *is already reaching into the esky and he
                takes out another beer ready to sling it to her.
                She pauses, though.*)

NINA   . . . coffee, please, I think.

                (MATT *is thwarted.* DAVE *grins, gets up and
                goes over towards the bar.* LENA *chooses this
                point to move towards* MATT *for a quiet word.*)

LENA   (*to* JAKE) Listen, sweetheart, I just need to ask
                Matt something. I'll be right back.

                (LENA *and* DAVE *meet, and he suddenly clocks
                the shirt – his shirt. He stares, frankly, at her
                chest.*)

LENA   Something wrong? Or are you just counting them?

DAVE   (*covered with embarrassment*) Sorry . . . !

                (DAVE *scurries behind the bar and fiddles with
                the coffee machine.* LENA *sits next to* MATT *for
                a hissed conversation which no one else hears.
                She is quite cross.*)

LENA   Hey! What the hell happened to you then?

MATT   What?

LENA   I thought the idea was that you were going to
                catch us at it and then act all outraged.

MATT   Yeah, that's right, that's right . . .

LENA   Well, you've missed that particular boat,
                sunshine.

MATT   Really? Christ, that was quick! I haven't even
                seen you go anywhere near him.

LENA   Oh, we got to know each other out on the pitch
                earlier on. Actually, it was easy, in the end,
                because he's a nice lad and I do rather fancy
                him. He's got some incredible chat-up lines. I
                had to keep reminding myself he's married . . .

MATT   Out on the pitch . . . ?

LENA   But hey, look, I wasn't expecting to go quite so
                far. I thought you were going to interrupt us
                before we did anything.

MATT   (*baffled*) But when . . . ? Where . . . ? I've been
                watching him like a hawk . . .

                (MATT *looks over at* NIGEL. LENA *looks at* JAKE,
                *who then looks over with a huge grin on his
                face.* MATT *realises that his plan has come
                unstuck.*)

MATT   Aw no! You and him? Jake, you mean?

                (LENA *winks back at* JAKE.)

MATT   No! Not him! That's the wrong one! Nigel, I'm
                talking about. He's just a kid!

LENA   The one who went outside, you said . . .

MATT   No, no, no! He hasn't even got a vote!
                (*Scratches his head vigorously with both
                hands*.) OK, look, it's not too late. You can still
                pull this off. There's Nigel, there, look. Go and
                start talking to him.

LENA   Joking! Wait a minute, so if Jake's not the one
                you meant, then he's not married?

MATT   No, obviously he's not married.

LENA   So that stuff he said wasn't all a line?

MATT   I don't know, do I?

LENA   So that really was his first . . . ? Oh my.

DAVE   Everything all right, you two?

MATT/LENA   Fine, fine, yeah, great, excellent, no worries . . .
                (*Etc.*)

                (*They are distracted – both have plenty to
                think about.* DAVE *wanders over to* NIGEL *and*
                NINA. NINA *is looking at the e-mail again,
                thoughtful. She folds it down to hide it from*
                DAVE *as he approaches*.)

DAVE   Still no word from Jo, Nigel?

NIGEL   Hmm? Oh, no . . .

DAVE   Ah . . .

NINA   That's sweet. With all that's going on you still
              remember to be concerned about Jo and the baby.

DAVE   Of course. And every time Nigel went out to
              talk to her on the phone in the first half
              England scored. He hasn't left the room since
              half time, and we haven't scored at all.

NINA   Hey, that's right.

NIGEL   I've told her not to call me until full time. I'm
              not missing anything else.

NINA   Apart from the birth of your first child, you
              mean.

NIGEL   Yeah, yeah, yeah . . .

              (NIGEL *concentrates on the screen.* LENA *and*
              MATT *hiss on.*)

LENA   (*hisses*) Well, it's bloody awkward. I come here
              to do you a frankly outrageous favour and
              suddenly find I've got myself a teenage
              boyfriend.

MATT   Just tell the kid it was all a big mistake.

LENA   With all the sensitivity of a rhino's arse, as
              usual. And don't even think of not keeping
              your part of the bargain.

MATT   All right, all right. Christ!

              (*On-screen, Johnson wins a throw against the
              head, to* NIGEL *and* DAVE'S *glee and* MATT'S
              disappointment.)

NIGEL   Yes, Martin Johnson! How many's that he's
              taken against the throw?

NINA   Quite a few.

DAVE   The man's a giant.

EXLEY   Well, it's got to help that there's another
               unfeasibly large bloke lifting him up in the air.
               That's not sport. That's a circus act, is that.
               That's It's a Knockout.

               (*On the screen, ref awards penalty to
               Australia.*)

NINA   No!

MATT   Ha ha!

EXLEY   What? What's happened?

NINA   Penalty to Australia. Kickable as well.

MATT   (*shouts*) Yes, come on Elton boy!

EXLEY   Why? Why is it a penalty?

DAVE   Offside.

NINA   Handling in the ruck. Vickery, look, there . . .

NIGEL   Oh, what's he doing, the bald buffoon . . .
               Doesn't he know this ref is just dying to give
               the game to Australia.

MATT   (*scoffs*) Yeah, that'd be right . . .

NIGEL   Watson's South African. It's a Southern
               hemisphere thing.

MATT   Yeah, the whole hemisphere's got it in for you.
               Here it goes . . .

NIGEL   Miss it, miss it, miss it, miss it . . .

               (*Flatley kicks the Australia penalty to make it
               14-11.*)

MATT   Yes!

NIGEL   Shit.

MATT   Great kick, mate, great kick.

NIGEL   Shit on toast.

MATT   14-11. Well, folks, it looks like the old Aussie
             double header might be on after all, doesn't it.
             The World Cup today, and then the election
             tomorrow. Whatever happened to that mad
             rush you were expecting at half time, eh?

NINA   Actually, Jake and I can clear up that particular
             mystery, can't we Jake?

JAKE   Um . . .

DAVE   What's that?

NINA   Why there's hardly anyone here this morning.
             It seems that someone sent an e-mail to all the
             members saying that the bar would be closed
             owing to damage caused by letting off the
             sprinklers last week.

DAVE   Who? Who did that?

NINA   Well, it's signed David Dowson.

             (DAVE *grabs the paper from her hand and
             looks at it.*)

DAVE   But I didn't . . .

NINA   Sent from the office there, five o'clock Tuesday
             afternoon. Were you in the office on Tuesday
             afternoon, David?

DAVE   Yes, but I didn't send this. Why would I? I was
             banking on the bar being crammed, bumper bar
             takings, impressing the committee . . .

NIGEL   I didn't get any e-mail.

NINA   Neither did I, but why not? Because you and I
                are "undecideds", that's why. The e-mail is for
                our benefit, so we can come along, see the bar
                deserted, and start to get the sneaking feeling
                that Dave isn't up to the job any more.

MATT   Don't look at me, mate. I was in Leeds on
                Tuesday. It's true, I was picking up a walking
                machine for the fitness centre.

JAKE   Anyone could have left it in the Outbox so it
                went when Mr Dowson – when Dave –
                switched the computer on.

MATT   Oh, like who?

JAKE   Dunno. (*When* MATT *turns away.*) Rebbit, rebbit.

MATT   Look. I . . .

NIGEL   (*suddenly points accusingly at* MATT) Toad!

MATT   Look, I don't know anything about any e-mail,
                and I don't know anything about any plan to
                make David look bad . . .

DAVE   (*eureka*) Veggie barbie.

MATT   What?

DAVE   Veggie barbie! The place is as quiet as a veggie
                barbie! I asked you whether that was authentic
                Aussie slang and you said you'd made it up
                yourself on the way over.

MATT   So what?

DAVE   Incredible. In-credible . . . !

                (DAVE *glares witheringly at* MATT *and then
                storms into the changing room.*)

NINA   So how did you know the place was going to
                be quiet? That's the point.

MATT   Nice try, Miss Marple. (*Beat.*) Ooh! Good
                  tackle, mate.

                  (MATT *sits, smug. The others glare at him.*)

EXLEY   (*into recorder*) "Midway through the second
                  half, the club became embroiled in a Watergate-
                  style scandal" . . . what's it going to be?
                  Something gate . . .

JAKE   I didn't know you were going to do that.

NINA   (*shrugs*) Neither did I.

JAKE   Do you think he's all right?

                  (JAKE *makes to go to the changing room.* NINA
                  checks him.)

NINA   I'll go.

                  (NINA *follows* DAVE *into changing room.*)

EXLEY   Veggie barbie . . . gate. No, that's terrible.

                  (NIGEL *glares at* MATT, *who watches screen
                  innocently.*)

NIGEL   That was a dirty rotten trick.

MATT   Nothing to do with me, mate.

NIGEL   You're quite a piece of work, aren't you?

MATT   Oh grow up.

NIGEL   Oh so you're admitting it now, are you?

MATT   I'm admitting nothing.

NIGEL   Yeah, well, excuse me.

(NIGEL *pointedly puts the can of beer that*
MATT *threw him earlier onto* MATT's *table, and*
goes over to sit at the bar.)

EXLEY   So we'll put him down as a don't know, still,
                 shall we?

MATT   Very funny. You're hilarious.

EXLEY   Still thinking you can win without my help?

                 (EXLEY *goes outside. After a moment or two's*
                 consideration, MATT *follows. Lights out in*
                 bar, up in changing room.)

                          Scene Two

Lights up on the changing room. DAVE *sits with his head in*
his hands. NINA *breaks the silence.*

NINA   So you think Matt knew about this e-mail,
                 then?

DAVE   Of course he knew about it. He's done it to
                 make me look bad. I don't know, maybe I've
                 been chairman long enough.

NINA   Well, if it is affecting your health.

DAVE   Where did you get that idea from?

NINA   Jake told me you were in hospital. He didn't tell
                 me why.

DAVE   He doesn't know why.

NINA   You're right, it's nobody's business but yours.

DAVE   All right, listen. Just between you and me,
                 right? I don't want you to have the idea that
                 I'm not up to the job. February it was. I was
                 woken up in the night by the most tremendous
                 pain, here. Awful. I was bent double on the

floor, couldn't move, couldn't get my breath. Sarah called for an ambulance, and they got me to hospital, knocked me out, did some tests. The first thing the doctor said to me when I woke up was, "Your drinking days are done, Mr Dowson."

NINA   What was it? Liver?

DAVE   Something called pancreatitis.Basically your insides start digesting themselves.

NINA   Christ!

DAVE   And for a while, until it settled down, they didn't know whether I'd only be able to eat mushed up food through a straw, but now they reckon I should be fine as long as I never touch another drop of alcohol as long as I live.

NINA   But you feel all right, though?

DAVE   Oh yes. Lost a bit of weight, actually. Maybe it digested itself.

NINA   Perhaps you should tell Jake, you know, what you've told me.

DAVE   Do you think?

NINA   He's worried about you, and it must be more worrying, mustn't it, not to know what was up with you . . . ?

DAVE   He's a good lad.

(*Lights out, back to bar.*)

Scene Three

NIGEL, LENA, *and* JAKE *in the bar.* MATT *and* EXLEY *have gone outside.* NIGEL *wanders back to his seat.* JAKE *grins a soppy grin at* LENA *as she comes back over to the bar.*

JAKE   Hi.

LENA   Hi.

JAKE   You all right?

LENA   Fabulous.

JAKE   I wanted to ask you something . . .

LENA   Yeah, look before you do . . .

JAKE   And I'm really nervous about it, which is daft,
            isn't it, because it's not as if . . . I mean, we're
            not . . . I mean, we've kind of broken the ice,
            haven't we . . . ?

LENA   We have rather.

JAKE   So I was wondering about later on, maybe we
            could . . . I don't know what . . . I mean, what
            would you like to . . . ?

LENA   Let me just stop you there, because there's
            something I really ought to mention . . .

            (NIGEL, *excited by a passage of play, gets to
            his feet.*)

NIGEL   Here we go, here we go, come on lads, this is
            better, drop goal Jonny Wilkinsaaan . . . ! (*More
            surprised than disappointed.*) Oh . . . ! (*Sits
            back down.*) At least we got into their half for
            once. What the hell happened at half time, eh,
            Wilko?

JAKE   Nothing happened at half time.

NIGEL   No, I mean, Jonny Wilkinson, look at him. He's
            shot. I think he looks shagged.

JAKE   Shagged?

NIGEL   He's got a sort of glazed look in his eye, look at him. Christ, he looks positively post-coital. Give the boy a cigarette . . .

JAKE   (*stares at the screen, appalled*) No. No, no, no . . .

LENA   Jake . . . ?

JAKE   (*to himself*) No, no, no, no, no . . .

NIGEL   Shagged.

JAKE   It can't be.

NIGEL   Shagged.

JAKE   I score he scores. I score he scores . . . !

NIGEL   Maybe he'll take him off.

JAKE   He wouldn't take Wilko off, would he?

NIGEL   He would.

JAKE   Who, Woodward? Woodward would?

NIGEL   (*nods*) Woodward would.

JAKE   (*disbelieving*) Woodward?

NIGEL   Woodward. Woodward would.

          (LENA *shakes her head, as if to clear it.*)

JAKE   You all right, Lena?

LENA   Yeah. I thought for a moment I was having a stroke.

NIGEL   Absolutely totally and utterly shagged.

JAKE   Will you stop saying that!

          (JAKE *heads outside.*)

NIGEL   What's up with him?

(LENA *shrugs.* MATT *and* EXLEY *come back in.* MATT *seems chuffed – they have completed their transaction.*)

MATT   What's the score, Nige?

NIGEL   14–11 still.

MATT   How long to go?

NIGEL   Few minutes. If the screen was the right size, obviously, we'd be able to see the clock.

MATT   Not to worry. First order of business when I'm chairman – buy a new screen. Come on Aussie!

     (*He winks confidentially at* EXLEY, *who is changing the tape in his tape machine.*)

Scene Four

Back in the changing room. DAVE *and* NINA *continue.*

DAVE   I came home one evening – Sarah was out – and the little leaded window by the front door was broken, and I must have forgotten to do the Chubb, because someone had obviously got in. So I went in, double locked the door behind me, and shouted for the bastard to come out.

NINA   Yes, not exactly what the neighbourhood watch recommends, but still.

     (*A lighting change lights up another part of the stage, and* DAVE *steps into a flashback as he is relating this incident.* NINA *listens as though he is still in the changing room telling this story to her. A hooded youth appears on cue, and sidesteps* DAVE, *then tackles him, as described below, and he turns out to be* JAKE, *obviously.*)

DAVE   So this youth appears out of the shadows at
              the far end of the hall, with his hood pulled
              right down so I can't see his face. And he's
              got a kind of duffle bag under his arm, and
              suddenly he runs at me. The hallway's only
              this wide, but as I'm about to smother him, he
              does a little jink left and suddenly he's gone
              right, and I'm tackling the telephone table. He
              gets to the front door, only I've done the
              Chubb behind me and it's a dead end. By now,
              I'm back on my feet, and I say to him, "Show
              me that again." Well, he hunches over and
              makes another run at me. I'm watching for the
              jink this time, but he just hits me, bang, and it
              was like being hit by a truck. I've gone flying
              backwards, halfway up the stairs, all the wind
              knocked out of me. Half a minute later – longer,
              I don't know – I open my eyes and he's there,
              peering down at me, making sure I'm all right,
              you see. He tries to dart away but I grab hold
              of him and his hood goes back, I see his face,
              and he knows it doesn't matter if he gets away
              now, 'cos we recognise each other. From school.

NINA   Jake. (DAVE *nods*.) So, what, you call the police?

              (*Lighting changes back, and* DAVE *returns to
              the changing room to continue conversation
              with* NINA.)

DAVE   No, no, no, no. I sit him down in the kitchen
              and we have a bit of a chat. Turns out he's
              never even played rugby, and, well, I've played
              with some bloody decent players in my time
              and I've never seen a sidestep like the one he
              pulled on me, and he tackles like a bag of
              cement. So I made a deal with him. Come down
              the club with me and give it a try – and,
              obviously, pack in burgling people's houses –
              and, well you can see for yourself how he took
              to it. And wouldn't it be great if he could win
              us a trophy, eh? You know, you've done it. No
              one can take it away from you, that.

NINA   No, they can just hide it away behind the big
                television screen.

DAVE   You know, I never used to think much of the
                idea of sportsmen being role models for young
                people, but since Jake has started looking up
                to Jonny Wilkinson he's really sorted himself
                out.

NINA   Shall we go and see how he's getting on?

DAVE   Jake? Do you know I've got a feeling he's
                doing OK for himself.

NINA   Jonny Wilkinson, I meant.

                (DAVE *grins, and the two of them go through to
                the main room again.*)

Scene Five

Back in the bar. NIGEL *is getting agitated at the game.* DAVE
goes to watch game, NINA *to the bar.*

NIGEL   Can you believe this referee? What's got into
                him?

MATT   Oh, here we go, it's the whinging Poms again.

NIGEL   No one's whinging, it's just . . .

MATT   You can't help it, I know. It's your national
                characteristic. Like ours is winning. We win –
                you whinge.

NIGEL   I can't believe you, I really can't. I don't know
                anybody who whinges as much as you. Oh, it's
                too cold, it's too hot, the beer's too warm, the
                backs don't tackle hard enough. You whinge
                from dawn to bloody dusk, all day long. And
                then when one of us makes an innocent little
                comment about something, out it comes –

Yaaah, you whingers, you whinging bladdy Poms! You whinge more than anyone. You even whinge about how much you imagine we whinge. You say the word whinge so often that it doesn't even mean anything anymore.

MATT (*beat*) Bloody hell, what a whinge! (*To* LENA.) Did you hear that?

(NINA *is over at the bar getting herself a drink.* LENA *takes the opportunity to join her and introduce herself.*)

LENA So are these guys for real then or what?

NINA I'm sorry?

LENA Look at them all, I mean, they're so into it. I like sport, I like games, but to do, to take part in. I can't get that worked up about watching. I guess it's a male thing, is it?

NINA (*suddenly rushes towards screen, points and shouts*) That's a penalty! Come on you bastard, what the hell's going on down there?!

NIGEL Oh, come on!

(DAVE *and* NIGEL *up on their feet, too,* MATT *sits back, shakes his head, smirking.*)

NINA Sorry, what were you saying?

LENA Doesn't matter. (*Suddenly tries to confide.*) I've . . . done something really dumb . . .

DAVE We're not actually going to do it, are we? How does it go, that Three Lions thing? Thirty years of hurt?

NINA Thirty-seven now, of course.

DAVE Although between '66 and '70 we were World Champions, weren't we? So the hurt didn't actually kick in until 1970, which is only thirty-three years. Of hurt.

NINA   Actually, England won the women's rugby world cup in 1994, so in fact it's only nine years of hurt . . . (*No one notices what she says.*) Hallo . . . ?

DAVE   Mr Exley? I was wondering whether, in the light of the revelation we heard just now, I could prevail upon you to . . . or rather not to . . .

EXLEY   Not to write that the place was as quiet as the grave owing to some sort of admin cock-up? I'm sorry, Dave, there is such a thing as journalistic integrity, you know.

DAVE   All right, then, a hundred pounds.

            (EXLEY *treats it as another joke, but* DAVE *was serious.*)

EXLEY   Ha ha ha. Good one. Hey, we might actually do this, you know.

DAVE   Oh it's "we", now, is it?

EXLEY   Well, we're just about to win something, aren't we . . . ?

DAVE   Wood, wood, touch some wood.

            (*Very tense.* NIGEL *imploring the referee's hooter to blow for full time,* MATT *urging one last effort from Australia.*)

NIGEL   Come on . . .

MATT   Come on . . .

NIGEL   Blow . . .

MATT   Push . . .

NIGEL	Blow . . .
MATT	Push . . .
NIGEL	Come on . . .
MATT	That's it, you're doing great. And again, push . . .
NINA	(*to* NIGEL) You should take Matt with you to the maternity ward, you know. He could really come in handy.
NIGEL	Eh?
MATT	One big push, come on, you can do it . . .
NIGEL	Blow you bastard . . .
	(*The South African ref does blow – for an Australian penalty*.)
MATT	(*exultant*) Ha ha!
NIGEL	No! What for? What's that for?
	(NINA, DAVE *and* JAKE *also take this badly*.)
MATT	I haven't a clue, mate, but it's a penalty to us.
EXLEY	I knew it, I knew they'd fuck it up.
NIGEL	What did I tell you? It's that referee. There's nothing there, nothing there at all!
	(DAVE *looks around at their appalled faces, tries to rally them*.)
DAVE	Hey, come on, he hasn't scored it yet. If he misses this England win, and even if he gets it it's still only level. Chins up, come on . . .
MATT	Here we go . . . Ye-e-e-e-s!

(*On-screen: Flatley scores the kick. English hands fly to heads in horror.*)

DAVE   OK, so now he has scored it, and now it's extra time, but we can still do this.

(MATT *gets himself a beer. Everyone else stunned, silent. Then* NIGEL'S *phone rings – he answers angrily.*)

NIGEL   (*into phone*) What do you mean where am I? I'm at the club . . . Well, no, not yet, aren't you even watching the game? It's extra time now . . . No, no, if there's an ambulance there then go in it . . . Well, what do you want me to do? Am I a midwife? Am I a qualified obstetrician? Just get on with it, can't you? . . . Don't cry, what are you crying for? . . . Well, you were the one who wanted the little fucker!

(*He hangs up. The others gape, open-mouthed with horror.*)

NIGEL   What?

DAVE   (*beat*) All right, hey, who wants a sandwich, then, eh?

(*Depressed and mumbled rejections of this offer.* NIGEL *slumps into a chair by* NINA. NINA *shakes her head sadly.* JAKE *sits with his head in his hands.*)

NIGEL   I don't get it. What went wrong in that second half?

DAVE   Come on Jake, chin up, son.

JAKE   We're going to lose, and it's all my fault.

NINA   It looked like Jonny Wilkinson just ran out of gas.

JAKE   Yeah, that's right, and it's all my fault.

DAVE	No, no, no, how can you blame yourself . . . ?
NINA	Why, what did you do? Step on a black cat?
JAKE	It is, it's my fault.
LENA	Oh come on, Jake, how can it be your fault?
	(JAKE *looks at her. He doesn't really want to say, but does.*)
JAKE	Because . . . you know how I have modelled myself on Jonny Wilkinson?
NIGEL	So?
JAKE	Well, for a while now, every time Jonny Wilkinson has taken an important place kick for England, I've gone out there and taken the same kick, the exact same kick . . .
DAVE	Well that's just a superstition. It's harmless.
JAKE	No . . . there's a bit more to it than that.
EXLEY	What do you mean?
JAKE	It's like this. When I score . . . Jonny scores.
	(*Beat.*)
MATT	Get out of here.
JAKE	It's true. When I score, he scores. When I fluff it, he misses.
MATT	It's coincidence. That's all.
JAKE	That's what I thought, at first, but it works every time. Like so far today I've nailed all four penalties and missed the conversion, and Jonny's done exactly the same.

DAVE
So that's five coincidences, and that's just today. How long has this been happening?

JAKE
Since the start of the World Cup.

DAVE
Since the start of the World Cup, so God knows how many coincidences that adds up to.

JAKE
Seventy-three.

NIGEL
Seventy-three? Jesus!

DAVE
Seventy-three? Seventy-three times you've kicked at the same time as Jonny with the same result?

JAKE
Yeah. It's like we've got some sort of psychic link thing going on.

(EXLEY *whistles the "X-Files" theme softly to himself.*)

NINA
There has to be some sort of rational explanation . . . I mean, you're a great kicker, and obviously Jonny's a great kicker, so the chances must be quite high of getting the same result . . .

DAVE
Seventy-three times in a row . . .

NINA
(*less certain*) Seventy-three times in a row.

EXLEY
(*speaks into his recorder*) "The tale I have to tell is a strange one, of a psychic link between two young men at opposite ends of the earth . . ."

NINA
You're not writing about this.

EXLEY
Oh, I think I am.

NINA
You're not.

DAVE
But Jake, I don't understand. Why is it your fault if Jonny went off the boil in the second

half? You didn't miss any penalties – we didn't even have any penalties.

JAKE   Well . . . the thing is . . . at half time . . .

MATT   (*gets it first*) You scored! That's it, isn't it? You scored at half time! Oh, that's fantastic! Ha ha ha ha!

NIGEL   Scored? What are you talking about?

MATT   He scored, the lad scored. In the showers, with Lena!

EXLEY   Oho . . . !

LENA   Thanks for that.

MATT   And he thinks that because he scored, Jonny scored, which is why he's been walking round like a zombie out there.

DAVE   No. But that's . . . No . . . I mean . . .

NINA   You don't really think . . . ? No . . .

NIGEL   You know he did look off the pace in that second half.

NINA   Did he?

NIGEL   Like he had a . . . groin strain, or something.

MATT   Ha ha ha ha! Well done, darling, you've performed a vital service for your country. You should get a medal or something. You deserve it every bit as much as those guys wearing the gold and green . . . (*Kisses* LENA.)

LENA   Hey, give it a rest, can't you?

MATT   Hey, and they don't know the best bit, do they? Because you weren't even supposed to

have it off with him. It was supposed to be
Nigel. Ha ha ha . . . !

LENA   Oh, great.

DAVE   What do you mean it was supposed to be
            Nigel?

MATT   (*suddenly realises he shouldn't have said that*)
            Um . . . nothing.

LENA   Oh come on, you may as well tell them now.
            Tell them. You brought me here with you so
            that I could get off with Nigel, you could catch
            us at it, and threaten to dob him into his wife if
            he didn't vote for you.

            (*A stunned silence while people take this in.*
            EXLEY *cackles to himself as he scribbles this
            down.*)

NIGEL   Is that offer still on the table? Because, you
            know . . .

MATT   I think the moment's passed, mate.

NINA   You were supposed to get off with Nigel?

LENA   Yeah.

NINA   So why didn't you?

LENA   Because cross-eyes here pointed out the wrong
            guy to me.

            (JAKE, *appalled, runs outside.* EXLEY *cackles,
            fit to burst.*)

LENA   See what you've done now? Jake, wait a minute
            . . . (*Runs out, too.*)

EXLEY   Well! Forget the other stuff. That's the story
            right there.

NINA   You can't.

EXLEY   Can't I?

DAVE   They've started again. Extra time.

MATT   You don't believe all that, do you?

DAVE   I'll tell you what I don't believe. I don't believe
               you'd try and win the election by blackmailing
               the first team captain in some sort of half-arsed
               sex scandal.

NIGEL   It probably would have worked, though, actually.

NINA   But you don't really believe that there's some
               sort of psychic link between Jake and Jonny
               Wilkinson. He scores, Jonny scores?

EXLEY   After all the things you've seen, Scully, why is
               it still so difficult to believe?

NINA   Shut up, you.

DAVE   Hey, you know what, that's a penalty, has to be.

NIGEL   Yes! Penalty to England!

EXLEY   The truth is out there . . .

NINA   Will you shut up!

EXLEY   No, I mean . . . the truth is . . . out there.

               (*Beat, then they all break for the door.* EXLEY
               laughs at them as he follows.)

NINA/DAVE/   (*shout*) Jake! Jake! Penalty! (*Ad lib, etc.*)
NIGEL

               (*Blackout.*)

Scene Six

Lights up on the field. JAKE *is by himself, being a bit moody.*
LENA *enters.*

LENA   Jake . . . ?

JAKE   I thought you liked me.

LENA   I do, I do like you.

JAKE   Yeah, but it was Nigel you were supposed to like.

LENA   It's a ridiculous situation . . .

     (*Then all the others flood over breathlessly.* NIGEL *and* NINA *first, then* MATT, *then* EXLEY *and* DAVE.)

NIGEL   Jake! Jake! It's a penalty!

NINA   Fifty yards out, on the right.

NIGEL   About here, actually, this is quite good.

JAKE   I'm not doing it any more.

NIGEL   What?!

JAKE   I shouldn't have said anything. It's stupid.

     (DAVE *and* EXLEY *arrive.*)

DAVE   It's a tough one, Jake. Long way out.

NINA   He says he's not doing it.

EXLEY   Not doing it? Why not?

NIGEL   Hang on a minute, what happens if he doesn't kick?

EXLEY   He's got to kick.

NIGEL   But what if he doesn't?

NINA   Who knows? Jonny's leg might fall off. A meteor might fall on him.

EXLEY   Look here, kid. Just have a pop at it and I'm
             pretty sure I can make you a star. You don't
             even necessarily have to score, as long as
             Jonny misses as well . . .

MATT   Listen, if the boy doesn't want to do it, then
             we've got to respect that . . .

NIGEL   Yeah, you'd like that, wouldn't you, you'd
             really like that.

MATT   All I'm saying is that if he's decided that he
             doesn't want to mess around with forces
             beyond his comprehension, then that's his call.

JAKE   What? You mean you don't want me to kick?

MATT   I don't want you to do anything you're not
             comfortable with, son.

JAKE   You don't want me to, do you? Right, I'm doing
             it then.

EXLEY   Excellent!

DAVE   Good lad. This is exciting, isn't it . . . ?

             (JAKE *starts putting (mime) ball on the
             kicking tee.*)

DAVE   It's incredible to think, isn't it, that this kick
             could be the kick that wins the World Cup for
             England.

NINA   So, no pressure then.

DAVE   No pressure, no . . .

NIGEL   Come on Wilko, the whole nation is depending
             on you.

             (JAKE *steps backwards into position.*)

DAVE	Get into the zone . . .
	(JAKE *gets into the trademark Jonny crouch.*)
DAVE	Don't let anything put you off . . .
JAKE	Please!
	(JAKE *holds his hand up for quiet.* DAVE *zips his mouth shut.*)
DAVE	Quiet everyone, please!
	(JAKE *begins to shape up for the kick again.*)
DAVE	(*trying to be helpful*) Slight wind, left to right . . .
	(JAKE *exasperated, breaks and regains his concentration. Then, just as he is about to kick . . .*)
MATT	Why does he do that, do you think?
NIGEL	What?
MATT	That with his hands.
NIGEL	Because the real Jonny does it.
MATT	Yeah, but why does real Jonny do it? He looks like he's going to hit the ball with a baseball bat. Or like he's holding a little umbrella. And he's suddenly going to go: "I'm . . . sing-ing in the rain . . ."
	(*Deliberately starts a little dance walk which takes him right over the ball, to put* JAKE *off.*)
DAVE/NINA/ EXLEY/NIGEL/ LENA	(*variously*) Hey, hey, hey, out of the way now, come on . . . !
MATT	Ha ha ha . . . sorry mate . . . !

(JAKE, *self-consciously gathers himself again, and kicks. They all watch the flight of the ball.*)

DAVE   (*slowly*) That's . . . a . . . beauty!

            (*Cheering, clapping* JAKE *on the back, by* DAVE, NINA, LENA, *ad lib.* MATT *grimaces.*)

NIGEL   That. Is. Quality.

MATT   Shit!

            (NIGEL *falls to his knees, picks up the little kicking tee* JAKE *was using to kick from and kisses it.*)

DAVE   What is that now? 17-14? (*Checks his watch.*)

MATT   Might not be.

            (*After a beat, they all realise at once that they should go and see the telly.* DAVE, EXLEY, NINA, NIGEL *and* MATT *all race offstage, leaving* JAKE *and* LENA *alone.*)

LENA   Great kick. That was really great.

JAKE   Thanks.

LENA   Don't you want to see if Jonny Wilkinson scores as well?

JAKE   Oh, he will do.

            (*We hear distant cheer from others arriving at the bar.*)

LENA   (*looks off, laughs*) Amazing . . .

JAKE   Listen, if you don't mind, I think I should have that shirt back, don't you?

LENA   Oh. OK . . . Listen, with me and Nigel. It was
              never supposed to be, you know, what we did.

              (*They are swapping shirts back.*)

JAKE   No?

LENA   No, no, no. Oh no. Bit of a snog, maybe, and
              then Matt was going to interrupt us, and . . . it
              sounds so lame, now, saying it out loud, that I
              can't believe I said I'd do it.

JAKE   So why did you?

LENA   Well. You know the fitness centre where Matt
              works, where you saw me that time? I own it. I
              own the fitness centre.

JAKE   So you're Matt's boss?

LENA   I am. He made me promise not to tell anyone,
              but then, you know, he can't keep his big
              mouth shut, can he?

JAKE   He's embarrassed to work for a woman?

LENA   I guess. And . . . well, you know what he does,
              don't you?

JAKE   Personal trainer, he says.

LENA   (*amused*) Does he?

JAKE   Yeah, fitness, diet, exercise programmes, that
              sort of thing.

LENA   Oh, right, well that's sort of it. Sounds kind of
              cool, doesn't it?

JAKE   I suppose.

LENA   What it is, though, what he does . . . is
              Dancersizing.

JAKE   It's what?

LENA   Dancersizing. It's an exercise class for middle-aged ladies. Keep fit and dance.

JAKE   (*amused*) Dancersizing?! Matt?

LENA   Oh yeah. And he's a huge hit. Massive. It's hard work keeping fit, you know, and having a bit of beefcake up at the front to ogle at, well, it makes a big difference to my ladies. I've had to lay on extra classes, and we're picking up more biddies from all over town. The centre is in profit for the first time since I took it on, and basically it's down to Matt.

JAKE   Dancersizing?

LENA   Yeah. Now he says to me he's thinking of moving to this new place. So I say to him what can I do to persuade him to stay . . .

JAKE   And this is what he came up with? (*Nods.*)

LENA   Like I said, it's a ridiculous situation, and I'm sorry you got in the middle of it . . . Let me ask you something, though. When you said, out here, remember, that I was your inspiration. Did you mean that or was that just a line?

JAKE   What's the difference?

LENA   Why don't you ask me what you were going to ask me. Earlier on . . . ?

        (*Pause. Lights out*)

Scene Seven

In the bar. DAVE *and* NIGEL *are pacing nervously up and down as the game nears its conclusion.* MATT *is somewhat dejected over by the bar by himself.* NINA *sits, and can't help*

overhearing EXLEY, *who is on the phone, just completing a*
hard-sell of an article idea to a contact on a tabloid paper.

DAVE   Is that a replacement?

NIGEL   It's Leonard. Lord Jason. We are not worthy . . .

              (NIGEL *bows in obeisance at the screen.*)

EXLEY   (*on phone*) Yeah, seventy-four, seventy-four
              times. So look it's got sex, the supernatural,
              Jonny Wilkinson, and maybe England winning
              the World Cup . . .

              (NINA *grabs* EXLEY *by the arm.*)

NINA   Are you calling your paper? About Jake? You
              are, aren't you?

EXLEY   Hell no, my paper wouldn't touch something
              like this.

NINA   Unbelievable.

              (NINA *tries to alert* DAVE *and* NIGEL *to* EXLEY'S
              conversation, but they are wrapped up in the
              game.)

NINA   Are you getting this?

DAVE   (*distracted*) Sorry, what?

NINA   This. He's going to write about Jake in the paper.

EXLEY   (*on phone*) OK . . . OK . . . yeah, absolutely . . .

DAVE   About Jake?

NINA   About the, you know, he-scores-Jonny-scores
              thing.

EXLEY   (*on phone*) OK . . . (*Checks watch.*) OK, that's
              doable . . .

DAVE	I don't understand. What's that got to do with the club?
NINA	He's not writing about the club any more.
EXLEY	Yeah, great. Oh, and Andy? This will be a 'Mark Gabriel', OK? Later. (*Hangs up.*)
	(EXLEY *hangs up, and is greeted by a bank of hostility.*)
EXLEY	What's up?
	(NINA *tries to grab his tape recorder, but* EXLEY *spots* JAKE *and* LENA *returning from outside and darts away.*)
EXLEY	Ah! Here are the lovebirds. So, Lena, great news. I've had a word with a friend of mine, and I'm authorised to offer you five grand for a photo.
LENA	What of?
EXLEY	You, in a swimsuit preferably, or some lingerie. If you've got any topless I could probably get them to go to ten.
LENA	What in the name of crap are you talking about?
EXLEY	They'll put you in a panel on the front page, headline: "I shagged Jonny Wilko in the showers at half time in the World Cup final", see pages 8, 9, 10, 11, whatever, obviously when they look they'll find it's not actually Jonny Wilko it's this kid, but they've bought the paper by then, haven't they . . . ?
LENA	What paper?
EXLEY	Hey, Jake, I told you I'd make you a star, didn't I? You might even get a Richard and Judy out of this.

JAKE   I don't want to be in the paper.

EXLEY   Oh come on, son, everyone wants their picture
                in the paper. You'll have to get used to that,
                you know, if you're going to make it as a
                sportsman, as a number of sources have led me
                to believe you are . . . (*Indicating* MATT *and*
                DAVE.) In fact, I shouldn't be surprised if by
                this time tomorrow you've been tipped to be
                the next Jonny Wilkinson, or rather, dubbed
                the next Jonny Wilkinson.

JAKE   I don't want to be in the paper.

EXLEY   This is how it works, you see, son. First you're
                dubbed the next somebody, then with a bit of
                luck you become the somebody, then
                somebody else is dubbed the next you.

DAVE   Didn't you hear the lad? He doesn't want to be
                in the paper . . .

EXLEY   Along the way, of course, there's all sorts of
                possibilities. A golden bollocks period,
                everything you touch turns to gold, medals,
                caps. Ads for hair gel and crisps. Career-
                threatening injury, turns out all right though.
                Photos of you and your lovely fiancee on your
                holidays, followed by tearful split, my side of
                the story. Three-in-a-bed romp with a couple of
                hookers in a Travel Lodge somewhere. Brief,
                not particularly successful stint as a team
                captain on Question of Sport. Ads for hair dye
                and denture adhesive. Drink driving charge,
                leading to Christmas in jail. My drugs and/or
                gambling hell, I'm penniless, I've flogged me
                medals to buy meths. Liver transplant, the end.
                All part of being famous.

JAKE   (*horrified*) I don't want to be famous.

EXLEY   Yeah, course not. Everybody wants to be
                famous.

DAVE   What if we deny everything, all of us? Eh? You
                can't print anything without corroboration.

LENA/NINA   Yeah!

EXLEY   (*amused*) I can't?

DAVE   We'd sue for libel. Jake, Lena, the club . . .

NIGEL   That's right. The rusty shield of . . . something
                or other . . .

EXLEY   Nice try, guys, but I've got it all on tape. Jake
                saying he thinks he's Jonny Wilkinson . . .

JAKE   I don't think I'm Jonny Wilkinson . . .

EXLEY   Whatever, and the sex in the showers, and
                Matt saying he set the whole thing up to
                blackmail Nigel . . .

MATT   (*groans*) Unghhhh . . .

EXLEY   . . . and then everyone out there watching that
                ludicrous kick, you nutjobs, it's all here, and
                that's all the confirmation I'll need. It'd be nice
                to have a picture, but if you won't sell us one
                then I'll just have to get a guy here with a long
                lens to shoot you through a hedge or the
                windscreen of a car . . .

LENA   You rotten bastard.

DAVE   Calm down everyone, it seems to me that there
                is a perfectly reasonable solution to this whole
                problem.

EXLEY   OK, I'm listening.

DAVE   Right, OK, here it is. You give me the tape
                recorder, and we forget about the whole thing.
                How does that sound?

EXLEY   Yeah, mate, in your dreams.

DAVE   OK, let me put it another way then. You give
         me the tape recorder, and we will let you walk
         out of here without kicking three shades of shit
         out of you.

EXLEY   (*laughs*) You're threatening me, is that it? This
         is recording, you know, right now.

DAVE   Well, you know, that only makes me want it
         even more.

         (*A long pause, in which* NIGEL, NINA, MATT *line
         up menacingly behind* DAVE. EXLEY *makes a
         sudden dart for the door, which* MATT *and*
         NIGEL *move to block.*)

NIGEL   You were asking about what constitutes a
         penalty in the game of rugby union, Mr Exley.
         Let's say you were to try and run past us.

EXLEY   I'm not going to.

NIGEL   For the sake of argument. In that case it would
         be perfectly legitimate for us to do this . . .

         (NIGEL *and* MATT *suddenly both ram* EXLEY *and
         drive him back up against the wall. This is
         painful for* EXLEY.)

EXLEY   Ooooof!

NIGEL   . . . and form what's known as a maul.

         (EXLEY *grimaces, but doesn't give in.*)

DAVE   A stiff arm across the throat, though, that'd be
         a penalty.

         (NIGEL *jams a forearm across* EXLEY'S *throat.*)

EXLEY   (*choking*) Aaarch . . . !

DAVE   Or perhaps you'd like to have a go at one of
              those funny lineouts you were so amusing
              about earlier. Of course, the ceiling's rather low
              in here . . .

              (EXLEY *looks apprehensive. Suddenly* NIGEL'S
              *phone rings. He fumbles for it without taking
              his arm from* EXLEY'S *throat. During phone
              call* EXLEY *catches* NINA'S *glare.*)

NIGEL   Ach! Excuse me. (*Answers phone.*) What . . . ?!
              Look, you couldn't have called at a worse time,
              I'm right in the middle of threatening someone.
              I'll call you back. (*Hangs up, then to* EXLEY.)
              Sorry about that. Now what were we just about
              to do . . . ?

              (NINA *charges over and joins into the back of
              the maul.*)

NINA   Come on! One . . . two . . . three . . .

              (*The maul starts to hoik* EXLEY *up to bash his
              head on the ceiling. He caves.*)

EXLEY   (*still choking, to* DAVE) OK! OK! Here, here . . .

              (EXLEY *hands over the tape recorder.* DAVE
              *takes it, rips the tape out, and stamps it to
              pieces on the floor.* LENA *and* NINA *clap.* JAKE
              sits with his head in his hands. MATT *and*
              NIGEL *let* EXLEY *down. He rubs his ribs and
              neck gingerly and makes it over to a seat.*)

LENA   (*suddenly*) Look!

              (*Everyone remembers the match and rushes to
              look at the screen.*)

LENA   It's Prince Harry.

              (*No one else is impressed by this.*)

DAVE   It's all right, Jake.

JAKE	He could still write something, couldn't he?
DAVE	Oh, I don't think so.
MATT	(*offers* DAVE *his hand*) Nicely done, Mr Chairman. Almost makes me want to vote for you.
DAVE	But not quite, right?
	(*They all drift back to check on the screen after the excitement with* EXLEY.)
NINA	How long to go?
NIGEL	Dunno, can't tell with this . . . (*Gestures in frustration at the screen.*)
NINA	That lineout is an absolute shambles.
DAVE	Look at them, they're like kids scrambling for sweets.
MATT	Penalty! Handling the ball on the floor!
DAVE	Who?
NINA	Dallaglio.
NIGEL	(*disgusted*) Nancy Dallaglio.
DAVE	Jesus. I don't think I can stand much more of this.
JAKE	Are you all right?
DAVE	Yeah, I'm fine, fine . . .
JAKE	Sit down.
DAVE	In a minute. Let's just see this. (*Exhales heavily.*) Whew . . . !

MATT   Seventeen-all, this'll be seventeen-all if he
                nails this.

NINA   What happens if it's all square at the end of
                extra time, anyone know?

DAVE   Yeah, erm . . . More extra time, and then it'll be
                drop goals.

LENA   Oh Christ . . .

EXLEY   Like a sort of penalty shoot out, you mean?

DAVE   Yeah.

EXLEY   Great. England always win at them.

MATT   Here goes . . . Oh yes! Never in doubt!

                (*Englanders all stare dumbstruck at the
                screen for a beat.*)

NINA   I'll tell you this. Somewhere there's a kid who's
                modelled himself on Elton Flatley who's having
                an absolute blinder.

NIGEL   I can't believe it, I can't fucking believe it.

MATT   There's something terribly English about this,
                don't you think?

NIGEL   I can't fucking believe it.

MATT   The glorious near miss, the fall at the last
                hurdle, so near and yet so far.

LENA   All right, calm down. Bit of dignity.

JAKE   How long's left?

DAVE   (*checks his watch*) Don't know exactly. The
                little clock's off the top of the screen, you see,
                on the wall . . .

NINA   Yeah, yeah . . .

NIGEL   Oh for crying out loud! Give me a chair, I'll tell
                you how fucking long is left . . . !

                (NIGEL *grabs a chair, slams it down in front of
                the screen, clambers up onto it, and
                accidentally bangs his head hard onto the
                underside of the video projector. There is a
                loud bang as a bulb goes in the machine.
                Some smoke. All the lights in the bar go out –
                not completely dark, though, as it is daylight
                outside the windows. A few seconds of
                pandemonium.* NIGEL *falls to the floor holding
                his head.*)

NIGEL   Ow! Ow! Ow! My head! My shagbastarding
                head!

NINA   Are you all right?

MATT   The fuse, the fusebox . . .

JAKE   I've got it.

                (JAKE *goes to the office and finds the fusebox,
                off-stage.*)

NIGEL   Ow! Blood! There's blood!

NINA   Oh, you're such a baby. I'll get you a towel or
                something, hang on.

                (NINA *goes into the changing room.*)

                (JAKE, *off-stage, throws the trip switch and the
                lights come back on.* LENA *notices that* DAVE
                has collapsed on the floor.)

LENA   Oh my God! Look!

                (MATT *and* EXLEY *go to* DAVE.)

MATT   Dave! Dave, mate! (*To* LENA.) Brandy, get some
                brandy.

                (LENA *runs to the bar and pours some brandy
                into a tumbler.* MATT *supports* DAVE'S *head,
                pats his cheek.* EXLEY *takes* DAVE'S *pulse – he
                doesn't really know what to do.*)

MATT   Dave! Come on, Dave . . . Do you think we
                should call a doctor?

EXLEY   He's got a pulse, so . . . oh no, hang on, that's
                his watch.

                (JAKE *comes back in and sees what's happening.*)

JAKE   Mr Dowson . . . ?

LENA   Here . . .

                (LENA *pushes past* JAKE *and gives* MATT *a
                glass of brandy. He tips it gently into* DAVE'S
                mouth. Then a little more.)

NIGEL   Ow! Ow! Ow!

                (NINA *comes back in with a wet towel for*
                NIGEL'S *head – she sees that something has
                happened to* DAVE.)

NINA   What's up, what's happened?

EXLEY   Dave has collapsed. He's got a pulse.

NINA   What's that? Brandy? You can't give him
                brandy!

MATT   Why not? It's medicinal.

NINA   It's lethal. You can't give him alcohol, you'll
                kill him.

MATT   Naaah . . .

NINA   It's true, he's not been well, he's had this . . .
            pancreatitis, it's called. He can't have alcohol
            or he'll die.

MATT   Oh shit!

NIGEL   Hey, what about my bloody head?

NINA   Oh, here . . . (*She throws the towel to him.*)

MATT   Shit! I've killed him.

            (MATT *reels back from* DAVE *and* NINA *steps
            in.*)

NINA   Water.

            (LENA *goes to get a glass of water from the
            bar.*)

JAKE   He never said anything to me about having
            pancrea . . . tis.

NINA   He didn't want you to worry, Jake. You're like a
            . . . he thinks a lot of you.

MATT   Shit!

NIGEL   I think I've stopped bleeding, anyway.

            (LENA *gives* NINA *a glass of water, and she
            tries to pour a sip into* DAVE'S *mouth.
            Suddenly he splutters a bit and sits up.*)

JAKE   Dave!

MATT   Dave! You're all right! Thank Christ for that!

            (MATT *throws himself at* DAVE *and gives him a
            big hug.* DAVE *looks bewildered by this.* MATT
            disengages himself, a little embarrassed.)

MATT   I'm . . . relieved . . . that's all.

(DAVE *looks around at them all, a bit disorientated.* NINA *has the glass of water in her hand.*)

DAVE

What's this?

NINA

Water.

(*She hands it to him.* DAVE *drinks it all.*)

DAVE

Hmmm. Funny. Tasted a bit like brandy at first.

NINA

They . . . did give you some brandy.

DAVE

Oh? (*Realises implication.*) Oh.

NINA

How do you feel?

DAVE

Ummm. OK. Not bad.

NINA

Didn't the doctor say drinking alcohol would kill you?

DAVE

Could kill me, he said. There were no guarantees.

JAKE

Shouldn't you go to hospital, though? Just in case?

DAVE

(*starts getting up*) Well, perhaps. Let's wait till after the game . . . (*Notices there is no picture.*) Did we win?

NIGEL

The game! Where's the game gone?

(NIGEL *gapes at the screen, looking for the lost picture.*)

MATT

You've knackered the machine with your fat head.

NIGEL

What we gonna do? What we gonna do? It's a disaster! The World Cup final, the most important day of my whole life, and the bloody telly's blown up!

NINA   Radio.

NIGEL   Radio? It's not a radio!

MATT   Car. Car radio . . .

NIGEL   Right!

                (MATT, NIGEL *and* NINA *bolt for the door, as does* EXLEY, *who'd like to get away.*)

DAVE   Wait!

                (*They all stop in their tracks and look back.* DAVE *is looking up at the projector.*)

DAVE   It's just a bulb that's gone, I've got replacements in the office. Jake? Top shelf on the right. It'll only take a minute or two.

NIGEL   But we're missing it right now.

DAVE   I'm taping the whole thing, OK? All we have to do is sit tight for a few minutes till it's all over, and then we just rewind it and watch it as live.

NIGEL   As live?

DAVE   As live.

MATT   As live, that's not bad.

NIGEL   But it could be . . .

NINA   As live, Nige.

                (JAKE *comes back in with the bulb.* DAVE *is about to change it, but* JAKE *does it for him.* DAVE *goes to office doorway and checks video is still on after power outage.*)

JAKE   I'll do it.

NIGEL   But . . . but . . . what if Jonny gets another
                    penalty? (*Pointing at* JAKE.)

DAVE   Jonny'll just have to manage on his own, won't
                    he. All right, now let's all just sit quietly, shall
                    we?

                    (*Everyone obediently returns to their seats
                    and sits.* DAVE *looms threateningly over*
                    EXLEY.)

EXLEY   Hands on heads?

DAVE   That won't be necessary.

EXLEY   How long for?

DAVE   Well, let's see. There's extra extra time, that'll
                    be a few minutes, and some of those have
                    gone. Then drop kicks, which'd take a few more
                    minutes . . . So not long.

                    (*Pause. Thumbs are twiddled.*)

LENA   So, you're all going to sit here looking at the
                    wall until the magic picture comes back again,
                    is that it?

EXLEY   Yeah. Pretty much.

                    (*Suddenly* NIGEL'S *phone rings – Swing Low
                    Sweet Chariot – on table out of reach.*)

NIGEL   (*jumps*) Aaaagh!

NINA   Don't answer it.

NIGEL   You're right. Could be Ponce calling from
                    Sydney.

DAVE   It could be your wife, man.

NIGEL   Yeah. She wasn't even watching it, was she.

DAVE   You've got to answer it if it's your wife.

NIGEL   She might know who won.

LENA   (*stomps over and picks up the phone*) Hallo,
                 Nigel's phone . . . ? No, he can't talk at the
                 moment . . . Me? Oh I'm here with one of his
                 team mates . . . (*Winks at* JAKE.) So how's it
                 going . . . ? Really . . . ? I bet it does, yeah . . .
                 Hang in there . . . Oh, you don't know who won
                 the rugby, do you?

                 (DAVE, NIGEL, MATT, NINA, JAKE, *and* EXLEY *all*
                 cover their ears and go "aaaaaah! Not
                 listening, not listening!", etc.)

LENA   OK, bye then. (*As they all stare at her.*) Well,
                 that's a turn up for the book. (*Beat.*) She didn't
                 know.

                 (*All relax and go back to their seats. More*
                 thumb-twiddling.)

MATT   Could be over already, of course. George
                 Gregan could have the trophy in his hands
                 right now, doing an interview in front of one of
                 those ridiculous boards with all the logos on it,
                 getting a medal from the Prime Minister, big
                 grins on their faces . . .

NIGEL   (*suddenly cracks.*) I'm going. I've got to go.
                 My wife's pregnant, you know.

                 (NIGEL *makes a composed and slow exit, to*
                 general astonishment. Then . . .)

MATT   He's going for the car radio.

                 (MATT *dashes out to grab* NIGEL, *who is*
                 dragged back kicking and screaming.)

MATT   (*off*) Oh no you don't. I know you, you'll be
                straight back in and wreck it for the rest of us.

NIGEL   I've got to know what's happening . . . !

DAVE   Nobody. Is. Going. Anywhere.

NIGEL   What!

DAVE   We all stay. We decided. We stay, we wait, we
                watch it as live. Together.

NIGEL   You can't make me.

DAVE   You go, Nigel, and I'll strip you of the
                captaincy and you can rot in the fifths.

NIGEL   Oh yeah, right. That's not your call.

DAVE   I'm the chairman of this club.

NIGEL   Matt's the first team coach.

MATT   (*has now decided to stay inside*) That's right, I
                am, and if you go out there I'll strip you of the
                captaincy and you can rot in the fifths. Now sit
                down and shut your stupid mouth.

NIGEL   Oh! Well, that's it. I'm not voting for either of
                you. I'm spoiling my ballot paper, and I'll enjoy
                doing it.

MATT   Please yourself. I don't reckon I'm going to
                need your vote in any case.

NIGEL   Oh really?

MATT   (*takes out a piece of paper – a letter – and
                waves it in* NIGEL's *face*) Yes really.

EXLEY   Oh dear . . .

DAVE   What's that you've got there?

MATT   Oh, wouldn't you like to know?

EXLEY   Yes, well, perhaps the classy thing to do would
               be to have a quiet word in private.

MATT   Keep out of it, sticky beak, this has nothing to
               do with you.

EXLEY   Sticky beak?

MATT   I have here a letter to the chairman from the
               chief scout of the Newcastle Falcons . . .
               (*Reads.*) "Dear Mr Dowson, It was nice to meet
               you last weekend, and to have a chat about
               your outstanding young fly half, Jake Whittam.
               As you know, we were seriously thinking of
               inviting him for a trial with a view to offering
               him a professional contract . . .

LENA   Wow, Jake.

NIGEL   Hey, Wilko!

MATT   (*reads on*) ". . . but if his behaviour is as
               unsavoury as you described, then perhaps it
               would be better not to expose him to the
               pressures of life as a professional sportsman."

JAKE   What?

MATT   (*reads*) "It was difficult to believe some of it,
               but if, as you say, his violent conduct and his
               arrogant and unpleasant manner has cost your
               club a number of long-standing members . . ."

NIGEL   Hur hur.

NINA   What?

NIGEL   Long-standing members.

NINA   God . . .

MATT	(*reads*) ". . . then I must agree with you that he is not for us. As for the other things you mentioned – the thefts of members' property, money, credit cards, a car . . . (*Others react, baffled, shocked.*) . . . and the potential dangers of introducing him to a level of the game where random drug testing is standard – well, I think, thanks to you, we have had a narrow escape. Yours sincerely, etc, etc . . ."

(*There is a moment of stunned silence. JAKE glares at DAVE, and then heads angrily for the changing room.*)

MATT	You see, to me that has the ring of a letter of resignation.
DAVE	How could you . . . ?
MATT	How could I what? Play God with a young guy's future?
LENA	Is any of that stuff true?
DAVE	Of course it's not true.

(*DAVE gets up and heads for the changing room. They watch him go.*)

NIGEL	I don't get it.

(*NINA hands him the letter to read for himself. Lights out in bar and up in changing room.*)

Scene Eight

DAVE comes into the changing room. JAKE has taken the shirt off and is putting on a t-shirt from his kit bag now.

DAVE	Jake . . . ?

(*JAKE turns and throws the shirt at him.*)

JAKE   So we square now, right? For the burgling your
                house. I don't have to keep coming down here
                any more.

DAVE   Is that what you thought? You had to keep
                coming down here?

JAKE   Community service, innit.

DAVE   No. What are you talking like that for?

JAKE   This what I talk like, for real.

DAVE   (*sighs*) Listen. I'll call them, I'll write to them,
                Newcastle, I'll explain. It was all a practical joke
                or something, a forfeit, a drinking game. They'll
                understand.

JAKE   Don't bother.

                (DAVE *sits heavily, takes a deep breath and
                tries to explain.*)

DAVE   I'm afraid I've had a bit of an annus horribilis.

JAKE   What, as well as the pancreas thing?

DAVE   I mean the pancreas thing. Lying there, looking
                down at tubes going in and out of yourself, it
                makes you feel . . . mortal, for want of a better
                word. And then with my father going into the
                home, seeing him every day, great powerful
                man he was once, and he's shrinking away,
                hunched over in his wheelchair, bits of food all
                over him. Every time I see him, I find myself
                thinking, what have you done, Dave? What are
                you leaving behind to say you were here, to
                say you were ever here?

                (JAKE *shrugs.*)

DAVE   I've been a teacher for twenty-four years. I
                must have been responsible for the welfare and
                education of hundreds – thousands – of
                children during that time, and do you know I
                don't think I've made the blindest bit of

difference to any of them. Until you. You're the
first one . . . It's like I finally managed to pass
something on, my love for the game, for rugby,
like my father passed it on to me.

(JAKE *doesn't respond to this.*)

DAVE   You're a terrific player, and . . . I wanted us to
            win the league. That's it. I wanted us to win
            something. I never once got my face in the
            same team picture as a trophy when I was a
            player, or coach, so I wanted to do it as
            chairman. I knew that if you left that'd be it.

JAKE   (*concurs*) Serious.

DAVE   It's an achievement, a photo on the clubhouse
            wall, it's something, you know? Making sure
            there is still a clubhouse, that's another thing,
            of course. More than that, though. I just
            wanted you to stay. That's it. I wanted you to
            stay.

JAKE   You're not my dad, you know.

DAVE   I know.

JAKE   Passing stuff on to me, and doing stuff you
            used to do with your dad. It's creeping me out,
            man. (*Beat.*) How d'you know about me nicking
            the car?

DAVE   (*surprised*) I didn't. I made that up. I made it all
            up.

JAKE   Oh, right then.

DAVE   Why? You did nick a car?

JAKE   Nothing. Forget it, right?

DAVE   So? What shall I do about Newcastle, then?

JAKE   You want me to go now, is it?

DAVE   I want what you want.

JAKE   Newcastle? What'd I want to go all the way up
                there for? Do they even speak English up
                there?

DAVE   Not really, no.

JAKE   Be the new Jonny Wilkinson, that's it, innit?
                The old Jonny Wilkinson already plays for
                them, what am I supposed to do about him?
                This whole Jonny Wilkinson thing is messing
                up my head. You saw what they were all like,
                out there, when I took that kick. I don't need
                that pressure, man. Everyone needing me to do
                it for them. And what if I played for Newcastle,
                played for England, like Jonny? There'd always
                be people like that Exley bloke wanting to know
                all about me. Being famous, man, you can keep
                it. Not for me.

DAVE   OK.

JAKE   In fact, you know what? I'm giving up the
                stupid game altogether. Right now. What do
                you think of that?

DAVE   They'll never win it without you, you know,
                Nigel and the others.

JAKE   What's it got to do with you? You're not going
                to be chairman any more.

DAVE   (*miserable*) Well. It must be almost time to
                wind that tape back, what do you say?

                (*He goes back into the bar.* JAKE *follows but
                not for a defiant minute or two.*)

                              Scene Nine

DAVE *emerges from the changing room after heart to heart
with* JAKE. NIGEL *pontificates sanctimoniously as* DAVE *passes
by.*

NIGEL   I must say, Daveso, considering that you think of the boy Wilko as the son you never had, I don't think much of your parenting skills.

DAVE   What did you say to me?

NIGEL   I said I don't think much of your parenting skills.

(*Pause.* DAVE *turns to face* NIGEL, *in a dangerous mood.*)

DAVE   Do you know, the one real bonus of stepping down as chairman of this club is that I will no longer have to be nice to you, you cretinous baboon.

NIGEL   Eh?

DAVE   (*contemptuous*) The woman you love is about to give birth to a child, your child, your first child, and instead of seeing this as a joy and a blessing, to you this is an inconvenience, an irritation that interrupts you watching something on the telly.

NIGEL   It's the World Cup f . . .

DAVE   Don't you know, you half-wit, that some people hope and pray their whole lives for what you're about to have, and it'll never happen for them, however much they deserve it, or would be thrilled by it, enchanted by it. No, it's happening to you. A man whose idea of living a full life is to be there watching when somebody else achieves something. Your wife's having a baby, do you not think you should be watching that? I pity you, but not as much as I pity her, and the day I take parenting lessons from you will be the day I paint my arse blue and do a dance in Woolworths.

(DAVE *has built to a shout in* NIGEL's *face.
Then suddenly calm.*)

DAVE   Now. Would you like to watch the end of the
                game. As live?

NIGEL   (*little voice*) Yes please.

DAVE   All right then. (*Turns and goes towards the
                office.*)

NIGEL   Well. Where did that come from?

MATT   Did I hear you say you were standing down,
                then, Dave?

DAVE   (*heavily*) That's right. You win.

MATT   (*goes into a vigorous celebration routine*) I
                win! You hear that, you mugs?! You bludgers! I
                win!

                (MATT *grabs a can of beer frm his esky and
                runs out singing Waltzing Matilda at the top
                of his voice.* NINA *approaches* DAVE.)

NINA   I'm sorry, David. You understand I can't, I just
                can't give you my support.

DAVE   (*downcast*) That's all right.

NINA   But just because I can't give my support to
                you, doesn't mean to say that you can't give
                your support . . . to me . . . does it?

DAVE   You? Support you? What do you mean?

NINA   Well let me put it this way. Which would you
                rather have as club chairman? An Australian?
                Or a woman?

DAVE   (*pause while he thinks*) We-e-ell . . .

NINA   David?

DAVE   Hang on, hang on, don't rush me.

NINA   Let me make it easier for you. A woman?
              (*Indicates herself, smiling in a friendly
              fashion.*) Or an Australian? (*Indicates* MATT.)

              (MATT *re-enters, shaking a can of beer, which
              he sprays over everyone in the manner of a
              grand prix winner. They protest, try to evade,
              he chases, especially* EXLEY, *who is thus
              prevented from leaving.*)

MATT   Yaaarcgh! You fackin' bahstads! Come on,
              celebrate you buggers!

DAVE   Good point, well made. Do you really think you
              could beat him?

NINA   I could give it a damn good try.

EXLEY   Can we please watch the end of this game
              before somebody drowns?

DAVE   All right let's have some quiet. Qui-ET! (*There
              is quiet.*) If you'll all take your seats quietly . . .
              I'll start the tape.

              (*They all sit, even* MATT, *subdued by deputy
              headmasterly authority.* DAVE *nips into the
              office and switches the video on.*)

DAVE   All right, now this is starting from the point at
              which Nigel head-butted the projector, OK?
              Ready?

NIGEL   Start!

NINA   (*turns away*) I can't watch. I can't bear it.

              (DAVE *presses the button. Lights come on on
              the projector. They all watch the screen. At
              once* MATT *is filled with glee.*)

MATT   It's another penalty to us! Right in the last
                minute! Come on Elton Flatley! There it goes!
                That's got to be it, surely, there's no time to
                come back from that! That's the World Cup!
                Again! Business As Usual!

                (*All* – NIGEL, NINA, JAKE, DAVE *and even* EXLEY,
                are appalled.)

NIGEL   (*on his knees*) No, no, no, no, no . . .

LENA   Wait. That's the same kick. That's the same
                kick we just saw before the bulb went.

JAKE   It's still only seventeen-all.

DAVE   That's right. I think you're right.

NIGEL   No, no, no, no, no . . .

                (MATT *unloads another can of beer
                everywhere, especially over* EXLEY.)

MATT   Yayyyy! Here we go!

EXLEY   Stop it, stop it, it's the same kick, look, it's the
                same kick.

MATT   What?

DAVE   It is, it's the same kick

EXLEY   I'm soaked to the bloody skin here.

NIGEL   No, no, no, no, no . . .

NINA   Nigel, snap out of it. It's still seventeen-all.

NIGEL   No, no, no, no, no . . .

NINA   Nigel! Dave . . .

NIGEL   No, no, no, no, no . . .

(LENA *slaps* NIGEL. NIGEL *is stunned. Looks at* LENA. LENA *slaps him again.* NIGEL *draws back his fist and is about to punch* LENA. NINA *grabs his fist.*)

NINA   Nigel, it's still seventeen-all, that was the same kick we saw already.

NIGEL   Wha . . . ?!

NINA   The same kick. It's seventeen-all. Still a minute to go, then sudden death. OK?

NIGEL   OK! Come on lads! (*Getting into it, hunches over, mime ball under one arm, other arm out in front, handing off . . .*) Look at Johnson, there. We're pushing them back, we're pushing them back now.

(NINA *and* DAVE *lock on either side into a little mini-scrum unit.* EXLEY *makes to leave while they are distracted, but at the doorway he turns to look, is drawn in by the action on screen and locks on as well.* MATT *and* LENA *try to push them back.*)

NINA   There's still time to do it.

DAVE   Jonny's ready, look, he's in the pocket.

NINA   He can't have a go from there, it's too far.

NIGEL   Dawson makes a dart through, that's another ten yards.

(DAVE *takes the mime ball and breaks off from* NIGEL *and* NINA, *surging forward like real Matt Dawson is doing on-screen.*)

MATT   Noooo!

(MATT *tackles* DAVE, *holding him up, though he stays on his feet.* NIGEL *and* NINA *catch up and join* DAVE, *pushing* MATT *back.*)

Nigel   Push, drive, push, come on, closer, closer . . .

Nina   Give it to Jonny, now, he's in space, he's in the
             pocket.

             (DAVE, *representing Dawson, turns and spins a
             mime ball to* JAKE *who's free and clear
             towards the back of the room.* MATT *sees this
             and tries to charge the kick down, going over
             the back of a chair in the process.*)

Matt   Noooooooo!

             (JAKE *catches the mime ball and swings his
             right foot in a drop kick. As his foot makes
             contact with the imaginary ball, FX: a bang,
             like a rifle shot. A few flashguns go off, as in
             the stadium crowd. Into slow motion:* JAKE
             *watches the arc of the kick. So do the others.
             The moment is frozen as they watch the ball
             open mouthed on the screen. Each has a line,
             punctuated by crowd noise.*)

Jake   The ball is spinning end over end, heading
             towards the posts, and I'm thinking: What do I
             want to give this up for, this is great, this is
             fantastic . . .

             (*More crowd noise, then . . .*)

Lena   The ball is spinning end over end, heading
             towards the posts, and I'm thinking: There's
             not that much of an age difference, is there?

             (*More crowd noise, then . . .*)

Nigel   The ball is spinning end over end, heading
             towards the posts, and I'm thinking: I'm about
             to be a father.

             (*More crowd noise, then . . .*)

DAVE   The ball is spinning end over end, heading
                towards the posts, and I'm thinking: I wish my
                dad were here now.

                (*More crowd noise, then . . .*)

EXLEY   The ball is spinning end over end, heading
                towards the posts, and I'm thinking: (*Extremely
                into it now.*) Go on you bastard, go on you
                little beauty. Yeeeeeeeeearhghghsssssss!

NIGEL   My son could play for England, which would
                mean . . . free tickets!

                (*More crowd noise, then . . .*)

MATT   The ball is spinning end over end, heading
                towards the posts, and I'm thinking: Shit, I
                think I've broke my bloody arm or something . . .

                (*More crowd noise, then . . .*)

NINA   The ball is spinning end over end, heading
                towards the posts, and I'm thinking: Victory.

                (*Then the crowd noise builds to a mighty
                climax as the ball soars home and the winning
                score is made.*)

COMMENTATOR   (*voice over*) "He drops for World Cup glory . . .
                it's up . . . it's over . . . he's done it! Jonny
                Wilkinson is England's hero yet again . . . !"

DAVE/JAKE/   Yeeee-ee-eeahhh!
NINA/EXLEY/
NIGEL

                (*They celebrate, and* DAVE *turns to* JAKE *but he
                is not forgiven yet. Then they all quickly
                realise that it's not all over.*)

NINA   All right, come on now, just get the ball in
                touch.

NIGEL   It's time. Isn't it time? It's time.

DAVE   Must be . . .

EXLEY   Come on, blow the whistle you South African
                 bastard!

                 (*They look at him for a beat.*)

NIGEL   It's time. Gotta go, come on.

NINA   OK, we've got it! Catt's got it.

DAVE   Into touch Catty!

                 (*They watch as Catt boots it into touch, left to
                 right. Hooter for full time. Suddenly they don't
                 know what to do with themselves. They gape
                 at the screen for a moment.* MATT *is in a heap
                 on the floor. He struggles into a chair,
                 holding his damaged arm.* DAVE *comes over.*)

DAVE   (*right in* MATT'S *face*) You tossaaaarghhhh!!!

MATT   (*hurt*) Hey, that's a bit much, isn't it?

DAVE   (*immediately chastened*) Yes, you're right. I'm
                 really sorry.

NIGEL   My wife. My wife's having a baby.

NINA   You should go.

DAVE   (*to* MATT) What happened?

MATT   I just thought if I could charge down the drop
                 . . . I mean, if there really is some sort of
                 connection between him and Jonny Wilkinson.
                 I think I might have broke my bloody arm.

NINA   You daft bugger.

JAKE
But it wouldn't have made any difference, would it? It had already happened twenty minutes ago. We were watching it on tape.

MATT
Yeah, I realise that now. Now that the grinding together of my shattered bones has sharpened my thinking. Ow!

NIGEL
I'm going to the hospital. You'd better come with me.

(MATT *struggles to pick up his esky and coat. No one helps him.*)

MATT
Ow . . . ! Ow . . . ! Ow, ow, ow! Ow!

(*As* MATT *reaches the door,* LENA *turns.*)

LENA
Hey Matt? You're fired.

Matt
(*thinking she is joking at first, but then the truth dawns*) Ow! What a bastard bloody day, eh?

(NIGEL *and* MATT *head outside.* LENA *makes to leave too, with* JAKE, *who turns in the doorway and goes back to* DAVE.)

JAKE
Hey, when we win the league, you'll just have to sneak into the photo at the back while nobody's looking.

DAVE
(*grins*) When we . . . ? (*To* NIGEL.) You're going to the hospital? Hang on a minute. I'll come with you. Nina? Here, can you switch everything off and lock up for me?

NINA
Sure, but what are you going to do?

(DAVE *gives her a bunch of keys, then takes a can of beer, opens it, drinks it.* NINA *and* JAKE *particularly are astonished, half-try to stop him.*)

NINA   Dave . . . !

JAKE   What are you doing?

                (*They all watch, appalled, as* DAVE *finishes the
                beer luxuriously.*)

DAVE   England won the World Cup. If that isn't a
                good time to have your last ever beer then I
                don't know what is.

NINA   Are you going to be all right?

DAVE   I think so. Now let's go and get my stomach
                pumped!

                (NIGEL, MATT *and* DAVE *exit to go to the
                hospital.* DAVE *helps* MATT, *who groans.*)

DAVE   (*chattering excitedly*) You know this could just
                be the start. This group of players stays
                together, stays fit, and with Clive – Sir Clive
                now, of course – we'll be invincible for the next
                ten years. At least!

                (MATT *groans even louder.* JAKE *grabs his
                kitbag, and leaves with* LENA, *leaving* NINA
                and EXLEY *alone together.*)

                            Scene Ten

NINA *and* EXLEY *are left alone. They say nothing for a moment.*
NINA *starts clearing up glasses, shifting tables and chairs
back to the walls. Then . . .*

EXLEY   Nina. Nina pretty ballerina.

NINA   Don't.

EXLEY   You used to like it.

NINA   So Mark Gabriel, you've been clinically
                impotent for three years, is that right?

EXLEY   Here . . . (*Gives her a cassette tape.*)

NINA   You got him to say it?

EXLEY   Oh yeah. The developers who want this place
               had him in their pocket, and they've given him
               spending money to make sure it happens.
               They've promised him a brand spanking new
               fitness centre all of his own, part of the new
               complex, and what do you think he wants to
               call it? (NINA *shrugs*.) Life Gym. Life Gym, but
               not as we know it.

NINA   How much did he give you for Dave's letter?

EXLEY   Two grand. (*Shows cheque.*)

NINA   Whew!

EXLEY   I could have got more, I think, but you wanted
               it to happen during the game.

NINA   I should cash that as quickly as you can if I
               were you.

EXLEY   When are you going to break it to him?

NINA   Just before the vote, probably. So, you still
               think rugby's a stupid game?

EXLEY   Yeah, well, England have won the World Cup,
               so it's obviously not a proper sport. Spot of
               lunch? Old time's sake?

NINA   I'll be right out. Just got to lock up. Switch off.

               (EXLEY *heads out to car park.*)

NINA   Hey Exley?

EXLEY   Yeah?

NINA   Thanks.

EXLEY   My pleasure . . . Madam Chairman.

(EXLEY *goes out.* NINA *is alone, looks around. The crowd cheering swells. Suddenly she thrusts both fists up into the air in triumph. Blackout. Then, in the blackout, music: Swing Low Sweet Chariot starts, very loud. Lights. Actors come on for curtain call, the bowing, etc. It is like the medal ceremony at the end of the final.* LENA *and* MATT *are on the end, in Australia shirts.* MATT *has his arm in a a sling. Both look a bit fed up. Then the English line up, with* NIGEL *on the opposite end. A member of the audience is dragooned into walking along the line dishing out medals.* NIGEL *is at the end of the line. He is handed a swaddled newborn baby instead of the world cup.* NIGEL *lifts it above his head like a trophy. Music and cheering swells.*)

Blackout. The end.